CAMBODIA'S DESCENT: POLICIES TO SUPPORT DEMOCRACY AND HUMAN RIGHTS

HEARING

BEFORE THE

SUBCOMMITTEE ON ASIA AND THE PACIFIC

OF THE

COMMITTEE ON FOREIGN AFFAIRS
HOUSE OF REPRESENTATIVES

ONE HUNDRED FIFTEENTH CONGRESS

FIRST SESSION

DECEMBER 12, 2017

Serial No. 115–97

Printed for the use of the Committee on Foreign Affairs

Available via the World Wide Web: http://www.foreignaffairs.house.gov/ or
http://www.gpo.gov/fdsys/

U.S. GOVERNMENT PUBLISHING OFFICE

27–812PDF   WASHINGTON : 2018

For sale by the Superintendent of Documents, U.S. Government Publishing Office
Internet: bookstore.gpo.gov   Phone: toll free (866) 512–1800; DC area (202) 512–1800
Fax: (202) 512–2104   Mail: Stop IDCC, Washington, DC 20402–0001

COMMITTEE ON FOREIGN AFFAIRS

EDWARD R. ROYCE, California, *Chairman*

CHRISTOPHER H. SMITH, New Jersey
ILEANA ROS-LEHTINEN, Florida
DANA ROHRABACHER, California
STEVE CHABOT, Ohio
JOE WILSON, South Carolina
MICHAEL T. McCAUL, Texas
TED POE, Texas
DARRELL E. ISSA, California
TOM MARINO, Pennsylvania
MO BROOKS, Alabama
PAUL COOK, California
SCOTT PERRY, Pennsylvania
RON DeSANTIS, Florida
MARK MEADOWS, North Carolina
TED S. YOHO, Florida
ADAM KINZINGER, Illinois
LEE M. ZELDIN, New York
DANIEL M. DONOVAN, JR., New York
F. JAMES SENSENBRENNER, JR.,
  Wisconsin
ANN WAGNER, Missouri
BRIAN J. MAST, Florida
FRANCIS ROONEY, Florida
BRIAN K. FITZPATRICK, Pennsylvania
THOMAS A. GARRETT, JR., Virginia
JOHN R. CURTIS, Utah

ELIOT L. ENGEL, New York
BRAD SHERMAN, California
GREGORY W. MEEKS, New York
ALBIO SIRES, New Jersey
GERALD E. CONNOLLY, Virginia
THEODORE E. DEUTCH, Florida
KAREN BASS, California
WILLIAM R. KEATING, Massachusetts
DAVID N. CICILLINE, Rhode Island
AMI BERA, California
LOIS FRANKEL, Florida
TULSI GABBARD, Hawaii
JOAQUIN CASTRO, Texas
ROBIN L. KELLY, Illinois
BRENDAN F. BOYLE, Pennsylvania
DINA TITUS, Nevada
NORMA J. TORRES, California
BRADLEY SCOTT SCHNEIDER, Illinois
THOMAS R. SUOZZI, New York
ADRIANO ESPAILLAT, New York
TED LIEU, California

AMY PORTER, *Chief of Staff*   THOMAS SHEEHY, *Staff Director*

JASON STEINBAUM, *Democratic Staff Director*

———

SUBCOMMITTEE ON ASIA AND THE PACIFIC

TED S. YOHO, Florida, *Chairman*

DANA ROHRABACHER, California
STEVE CHABOT, Ohio
TOM MARINO, Pennsylvania
MO BROOKS, Alabama
SCOTT PERRY, Pennsylvania
ADAM KINZINGER, Illinois
ANN WAGNER, Missouri

BRAD SHERMAN, California
AMI BERA, California
DINA TITUS, Nevada
GERALD E. CONNOLLY, Virginia
THEODORE E. DEUTCH, Florida
TULSI GABBARD, Hawaii

CONTENTS

Page

WITNESSES

LETTERS, STATEMENTS, ETC., SUBMITTED FOR THE HEARING

APPENDIX

CAMBODIA'S DESCENT: POLICIES TO SUPPORT DEMOCRACY AND HUMAN RIGHTS

____

TUESDAY, DECEMBER 12, 2017

HOUSE OF REPRESENTATIVES,
SUBCOMMITTEE ON ASIA AND THE PACIFIC,
COMMITTEE ON FOREIGN AFFAIRS,
Washington, DC.

The subcommittee met, pursuant to notice, at 2:00 p.m., in room 2255, Rayburn House Office Building, Hon. Ted Yoho (chairman of the subcommittee) presiding.

Mr. YOHO. The subcommittee will come to order.

Members present will be permitted to submit written statements to be included in the official hearing record. Without objection, the hearing record will remain open for 5 calendar days to allow statements, questions, and extraneous material for the record subject to length, limitations, and the rules.

Well, good afternoon, everybody. And I can tell by the amount of participation in this room, this is a very important topic. And I want to thank you, the ranking member, my colleagues, and the panel for joining us today to discuss the events in Cambodia. We are holding this hearing at a consequential moment for Cambodia with serious implications for over 6 million of its citizens and for Southeast Asia and for democracy and human rights in the region. Cambodia is set to hold general elections in July 2018, which were predicted to be particularly significant for the country's progress toward genuine democracy. Recent elections, including the 2013 general elections and recent local elections, saw unprece- dented gains for the Cambodia National Rescue Party, a consoli- dated opposition movement.

Many observers believe that in 2018, the CNRP would win an unprecedented parliamentary majority. Unfortunately, Cambodia's authoritarian leader had other plans. Hun Sen, the sitting prime minister, has been in power for more than 30 years, and has no in- tentions of relinquishing power. In face of strengthening support for the opposition, it seems Hun Sen has decided that he can no longer dominate the polls, even in a rigged election system. He will retain power through force.

Over the last years, his brutal consolidation of powers played out on numerous fronts. Hun Sen has chilled support for the opposition by threatening to deploy the miliary if elections do not go his way, and has used his control of the government to dismantle threats to his grip on power.

Two years ago, two CNRP lawmakers were savagely dragged from their cars and beaten by Hun Sen's bodyguards. While the perpetrators served token sentences, they were promoted to colonel barely 2 weeks after being released. Such is the reward for crushing the opposition.

In early September, authorities arrested Kem Sokha, the leader of the CNRP, and charged him with treason, allegedly for participating in an American plot to undermine Hun Sen's regime.

Only last month, Cambodia Supreme Court dissolved the CNRP, again citing the party's involvement in an alleged U.S.-backed plot. The chief judge, who is an ally of Hun Sen, relied on legal authorities that were created by the regime's controlled Parliament this year to give the ruling party sweeping powers over competing parties. We are seeing this around the globe. One only needs to look at Venezuela, the same thing is happening there.

To dismantle Cambodia's only credible opposition came amid a slew of other actions to eliminate dissenting—dissent among civil society. In August, the regime shut down the Office of the National Democratic Institute, a preeminent NGO that is active in promoting democracies around the world. Other NGOs have been investigated and subject to increased scrutiny.

In recent months, the regime has forced the closure of independent media outlets that challenged its control over information, including Radio Free Asia, the Voice of America, and other publications and radio stations.

Hun Sen's corrupt, oppressive regime perpetuates a culture of human rights abuses and restrictions of political freedoms. As Human Rights Watch finds, his rule has relied on security force violence and politically motivated persecution. Security forces commit killings and torture with impunity. The politically powerful have carried out forced evictions and illegal land grabs for decades. And again, we are seeing this in other parts of the world run by other governments. Government officials and judges are mirrored in corruption.

Hun Sen's relentless consolidation of power this year means that these widespread abuses will continue. It goes without saying that this is an intolerable situation for the people of Cambodia.

The White House deserves recognition for taking decisive actions on these issues. In November, the press secretary issued a strong statement on the regime's action to undermine democracy. And this month, the State Department began implementing visa restrictions for officials involved in these actions, but more must be done.

The human rights and democracy in Cambodia have broad implications for the region and the world. Cambodia is a member of ASEAN, the premier international forum in Southeast Asia, with nine other nations, and accounts for 633 million people, and $2.5 trillion in trade. Every one of its 10 members must agree in order for the bloc to act, so any nation operating outside the bounds of humanity and decency will have an outsize effect on the entire group. This is such an important issue, not just for the Cambodian people, but for that whole region and, really, for the world.

Hun Sen and his cronies are also clients of China. Chinese aid increases Hun Sen's resilience to international pressure, perpetuates corruption within Cambodia, and gives China undue influence within ASEAN. China's support of Hun Sen's regime shows that its policy's priorities are dramatically out of step with global humanitarian norm, despite China's rapidly growing global profile.

It has been a difficult year for the cause of human rights and democracy in Cambodia, and the year ahead may even be harder. So in today's hearing, we will try to determine how Congress can best contribute to this cause.

I thank the panel for helping to guide us in this important work. And, without objection, the witnesses' written statements will be entered into the hearing record.

And I now turn to the ranking member, Mr. Sherman, for any remarks he may have.

[The prepared statement of Mr. Yoho follows:]

Cambodia's Descent: Policies to Support Democracy and Human Rights
Subcommittee on Asia and the Pacific
House Committee on Foreign Affairs
Tuesday, December 12, 2017, 2:00 p.m.
Opening Statement of Chairman Ted Yoho

Good afternoon, and thank you to the Ranking Member, my colleagues, and the panel for joining us today to discuss events in Cambodia. We are holding this hearing at a consequential moment for Cambodia, with serious implications for its 16 million citizens, for Southeast Asia, and for democracy and human rights in the region.

Cambodia is set to hold general elections in July of 2018, which were predicted to be particularly significant for the country's progress towards genuine democracy. Recent elections, including the 2013 general elections and recent local elections, saw unprecedented gains for the Cambodia National Rescue Party, a consolidated opposition movement. Many observers believed that in 2018, the CNRP would win an unprecedented parliamentary majority.

Unfortunately, Cambodia's authoritarian leader had other plans. Hun Sen, the sitting Prime Minister, has been in power for more than 30 years, and has no intentions on relinquishing power. In the face of strengthening support for the opposition, it seems Hun Sen has decided that if he can no longer dominate the polls even in a rigged election system, he will retain power through force.

Over the last year, his brutal consolidation of power has played out on numerous fronts. Hun Sen has chilled support for the opposition by threatening to deploy the military if elections do not go his way, and has used his control of the government to dismantle threats to his grip on power.

Two years ago, two CNRP lawmakers were savagely dragged from their cars and beaten by Hun Sen's bodyguards. While the perpetrators served token sentences, they were promoted to "colonel" barely two weeks after being released. Such is the reward for crushing the opposition.

In early September, authorities arrested Kem Sohka, the leader of the CNRP, and charged him with treason, allegedly for participating in an American plot to undermine Hun Sen's regime.

Only last month, Cambodia's Supreme Court dissolved the CNRP, again citing the party's involvement in an alleged U.S.-backed plot. The chief judge, who is an ally of Hun Sen, relied on legal authorities that were created by the regime-controlled Parliament this year to give the ruling party sweeping powers over competing parties.

The dismantling of Cambodia's only credible opposition came amid a slew of other actions to eliminate dissent among civil society. In August, the regime shut down the office of the National Democratic Institute, a preeminent NGO that is active in promoting democracy around the world. Other NGOs have been investigated and subjected to increased scrutiny.

In recent months, the regime has also forced the closure of independent media outlets that challenged its control over information, including Radio Free Asia, the Voice of America, and other publications and radio stations.

Hun Sen's corrupt and oppressive regime perpetuates a culture of human rights abuses and restrictions of political freedoms. As Human Rights Watch finds, "His rule has relied on security force violence and politically motivated persecution… Security forces commit killings and torture with impunity… The politically powerful have carried out forced evictions and illegal land grabs for decades. Government officials and judges are mired in corruption."

Hun Sen's relentless consolidation of power this year means that these widespread abuses will continue. It goes without saying that this is an intolerable situation for the people of Cambodia.

The White House deserves recognition for taking decisive action on these issues. In November, the Press Secretary issued a strong statement on the regime's actions to undermine democracy. And this month, the State Department began implementing visa restrictions for officials involved in these actions. But more must be done.

Human rights and democracy in Cambodia have broad implications for the region and the world. Cambodia is a member of ASEAN, the premier international forum in Southeast Asia, which operates on consensus. Every one of its ten members must agree in order for the bloc to act, so any nation operating outside the bounds of humanity and decency will have an outsize effect on the entire group.

Hun Sen and his cronies are also clients of China. Chinese aid increases Hun Sen's resilience to international pressure, perpetuates corruption within Cambodia, and gives China undue influence within ASEAN. China's support of Hun Sen's regime shows that its policy priorities are dramatically out of step with global humanitarian norms, despite China's rapidly growing global profile.

It has been a difficult year for the cause of human rights and democracy in Cambodia, and the year ahead may be even harder. So, in today's hearing, we will try to determine how Congress can best contribute to this cause. I thank the panel for helping to guide us in this important work, and will turn to the Ranking Member for his remarks.

———————

Mr. SHERMAN. Thank you. Thank you, Mr. Chairman.

Mr. YOHO. Do you want my gavel?

Mr. SHERMAN. No, no, you keep your wedding ring.

The mission of this subcommittee is so important that even another subcommittee is having hearings on Asia, namely, the North Korea hearings being held by the Africa and Human Rights Subcommittee.

Looking at this from a global standpoint, American resources are finite. We have a limited amount of foreign aid. We have a limited amount of preferential access that we can give to the United States' market, particularly with textiles. And if the Cambodian Government is unworthy of this, then perhaps we need to allocate it to poorer countries that are moving toward democracy.

In the past two decades, the United States has invested hundreds of millions of dollars in Cambodia to help it on the road of recovery and to rebuild after the costly civil war. The international community has joined us in efforts to rebuild the country and move toward democracy.

In addition to what we list as the expenses, that special access to American markets takes jobs away from Americans, takes jobs away from those in AGOA, takes jobs away from those in South Asia. Somebody is going to be making those garments, and that is an additional advantage we give to Cambodia.

Organizations such as the NDI, represented here, the International Republican Institute, and Radio Free Asia, have engaged with local Cambodian partners in building a capacity for civil society. Despite this, Cambodia has been ruled continuously by Prime Minister Hun Sen and the Cambodia People's Party. Now, they were willing to share power in a coalition for some years. Prospects for democracy, though, have suffered setbacks in the last 2 years because the government has adopted policies aimed at eliminating the opposition.

In 2015, the Cambodian Parliament passed the Law on Associations of Nongovernmental Organizations, LANGO, to revoke the registration of certain nongovernmental organizations. In August, Cambodia ordered the closure of the National Democratic Institute on the theory that it had violated LANGO. We have the president of that organization here, and you are to be commended for being effective, and that is why your organization was expelled.

The Cambodian Government has also ordered radio stations to stop broadcasting. Radio Free Asia and Voice of America, these are vital sources of credible independent information for the people of Cambodia.

Kem Sokha, the leader of the opposition, Cambodian National Rescue Party, was arrested just a few months ago on September 3, and charged with treason and with conspiring with the United States Government to overthrow the Government of Cambodia. We have with us Kem Sokha's daughter, Ms. Kem, who will be a witness at these hearings. And the dedication of your family to the people of Cambodia is exemplified by your father's sacrifice.

The CNRP's previous leader, Sam Rainsy, remains in exile. In November, Cambodia's Supreme Court ordered the Cambodian National Rescue Party to be dissolved. And I will point out that the charges against Ms. Kem's father are also charges against the Government and people of the United States claiming that we are trying to "overthrow the government."

The United States and our international partners must act quickly to stop this backsliding away from democracy. Toward that end, I have co-sponsored legislation with Congressman Lowenthal, the co-chair of the Cambodian Caucus, together with Mr. Chabot and others who are here.

Our bill supports the decision announced by the Secretary of State on December 6 to restrict entry to the United States for individuals involved in undermining democracy in Cambodia. And it urges the executive branch to consider placing all senior Cambodian Government officials implicated in the crackdown on democracy on the list of specially designated nationals so they are subject to travel restrictions and freezes.

We don't want to hurt the Cambodian people. We don't want to disrupt our investment in Cambodian society, but we do need to re-evaluate our foreign aid and our special access. And we need to turn to our European friends and remind them that they too could be providing special access to poor people in Africa or South Asia, or they could be working with a government in Cambodia that is increasingly authoritarian.

We strongly urge Cambodia's government to reinstate the political opposition, release Kem Sokha, allow civil society and media to resume their constitutionally protected activities, allow NDI back into Cambodia, and release former Radio Free Asia journalists who have been arrested on dubious charges.

If the Cambodian Government does not take these steps and does not bring Cambodia on the path to genuine democracy, it is hard to see how the United States and our international partners could accept the legitimacy of next year's elections, or continue the economic aid and concessionary trade that so many other people in countries that are moving to democracy have asked to be directed in their direction.

I yield back.

Mr. YOHO. Thank you for your comments.

And we have the honor and the great pleasure of having the chairman of the full committee, Mr. Ed Royce, to join us. So thank you, Mr. Chairman.

Mr. ROYCE. Thank you, Mr. Chairman. And thanks for holding this hearing today on an issue that really needs worldwide attention and needs it now. And let me say, you know, the demise of democracy in Cambodia, the ongoing human rights nightmare in Cambodia, the violations that the Hun Sen regime is committing against basic human rights and the rule of law, this is the reason for this hearing. This is why we are so discouraged, but our hearts go out to the people of Cambodia with all they have been through, and especially since the elections back in 2013.

We have seen such gross attacks on those Cambodians that peacefully oppose this growing authoritarian trend by the government. Hun Sen's regime, frankly, has become thuggish. It continues to crack down on the political opposition, arresting and beating those who speak out and oppose in any way they rule.

Freedom House, you know, does an analysis every year, and it consistently rates Cambodia now as not free, but that is putting it very mildly. Two years ago, opposition lawmaker and American citizen, Nhay Chamroeun, was severely and brutally attacked by plainclothes bodyguards. Most of the world saw the photographs in the paper about what happened. They repeatedly kicked and stomped him. He was hospitalized for months.

Several months later, Kem Ley, a popular Cambodian political commentator, was murdered in broad daylight. And why was he murdered? Because he had written. He had spoken out about some of these abuses.

And over the last few months, Hun Sen has dispatched any notion that democracy in Cambodia is going to continue to be maintained under their rule. They have dissolved the CNRP. They arrested its leader, Kem Sokha, who faces very spurious charges, obviously, by the government. And despite deep flaws in 2013, for those of us that were watching those elections, there were big gains made by the opposition in those elections. And since that time, we have seen a complete dismemberment of the political system in Cambodia. Make no mistake, the government is now run by an authoritarian thug. That is the unfortunate fact.

The Trump administration has responded with some positive steps: Last week's announcement of the visa ban on those undermining democracy. That is welcomed. But by no means should this be the last stop.

And I look forward to hearing from our witnesses on what additional measures we should take to support Cambodia's democracy. That is what we are calling—we are a democracy here, we are calling on other republics around the world, other democratic institutions. Now is the time to come forward.

And again, I want to thank the chairman for holding this very important hearing, Mr. Yoho, on a subject that demands, frankly, our attention, and doesn't get enough of our attention. So thank you again for doing this.

Mr. YOHO. Thank you for joining us, Chairman Royce. It is an honor to have you here. And we are also blessed to have Alan Lowenthal, not a member of this committee, but from California, but is very passionate.

And if I hear no objection, I will let him have 5 minutes.

Hearing none, Mr. Lowenthal, you have 5 minutes, and I look forward to your comments. And thank you for being here.

Mr. LOWENTHAL. Well, thank you, Mr. Chair. You know, I am very pleased that you called this timely hearing on Cambodia's dissent from democracy. And I also want to comment on Chairman Royce.

You have been a steadfast proponent and champion for democracy, and you have been part of—you have been calling for reforms and changes in Cambodia for many years, and so I want to thank you too.

You know, as we have already heard, the situation in Cambodia is dire. I am just going to go over a few things, and I think it is really important to say them again, because it is really important for the United States Congress and all those that are watching to understand the importance that we play on the situation in Cambodia today and why we are holding this hearing.

We are witnessing the death of democracy. You know, Cambodian democracy really began in 1991 with the Paris Accord, which called for democracy, which called for ongoing free and fair elections, which have not occurred. And now we are witnessing this death of democracy, not by a single action, but in 1,000 recent cuts and 1,000 attempts by the Hun Sen regime.

He has increased, as we pointed out, the intimidation against the opposition, CNRP. He has used political maneuvers to oust the former CNRP president, Sam Rainsy. He has arrested the current CNRP president, Kem Sokha, as we all know, and charged him with treason. And removed the rest of the CNRP from their posts in the Cambodian Parliament.

He began a crackdown on nongovernment organizations, the NGOs, and the independent media, all of this in anticipation of the election, to eliminate all public comment and opposition to the elections next year. And as has been pointed out, the National Democratic Institute, Radio Free Asia, and others were forced to cease operations.

Individuals related to the these groups were also arrested, such as two RFA reporters, who are now facing between 7 and 15 years in prison for charges of espionage. The arrest of Kem Sokha by the Hun Sen regime, who has sent—when he sent armed forces to raid Kem Sokha's house and arrest him without a warrant and led him away in handcuffs. And as we know, the fictitious case against Kem Sokha, the Canadian Government has implicated the United States as a co-conspirator. I think that is really important for us to understand, that we have been identified as a co-conspirator in Kem Sokha's alleged crime of treason to topple the Cambodian Government.

He is now being held in a maximum security prison near the border of Vietnam. And also what is very troubling is that China, in a very unusual step, weighed in publicly to support the arrest of the Kem Sokha. The Cambodian Supreme Court then ruled to dissolve the CNRP, and the Hun Sen controlled Parliament passed a rule, a law to redistribute the seats held by the CNRP to minority parties. Fifty-five seats were reassigned from the CNRP to these other parties. More than 5,000 commune councilor positions won by the CNRP in the June local elections were redistributed to other minor political parties or these people were forced to defect if they wanted to stay on to the Hun—become part of the Hun Sen party. This essentially ended all political opposition to Hun Sen.

Following these moves, it is to the White House's credit, that it announced that it would no longer support the 2018 election in Cambodia, calling it illegitimate. I think it is really critically important that we are seeing the lack of legitimacy on the part.

As co-chair of the Congressional Caucus on Cambodia, along with my other co-chair, Congressman Chabot, we have introduced a resolution, which is a companion resolution to the U.S. Senate passed McCain-Durbin resolution, which really cites the problems that are going on in Cambodia.

I think I would just like to close and say also, I am really here to understand what are the next steps that we must do. We must support the efforts of our State Department. We must continue to educate. We must make sure that Kem Sokha is released. We must make sure that the CNRP is able to be become a viable political party once more. But I think we also must, as Chairman Royce has said, we must look at ways to reach out to the world, to our EU partners, our partners in Japan, who are the big trading partners of Cambodia, and speak with one voice that the world will not allow Cambodia to dissent from democracy.

So I want to thank you, Mr. Chairman, again, for holding this hearing. It is critically important. You know, we spend time talking about crises in North Korea, in the Middle East; we are in danger, without looking at it as a specific crisis but an ongoing issue, of losing Southeastern Asia, and especially losing the one country that was moving toward democracy, which will now be lost. And so I am so pleased with you for holding this hearing, Mr. Chair. And I yield back.

Mr. YOHO. Well, I appreciate your comments and your input. We will now go to opening statements from members, Mr. Rohrbacher from California.

Mr. ROHRABACHER. Thank you very much, Mr. Chairman. Thank you for holding this hearing.

I have been deeply involved with this issue with Congressman Lowenthal and Congressman Royce. We have spent a lot of time and effort trying to do what is right over the years, and I don't think we have accomplished what we wanted to.

Mr. LOWENTHAL. It has gone in the wrong direction.

Mr. ROHRBACHER. It has actually gone in the wrong direction, like you say. I remember when Cambodia did have hope. I remember that after—we realized that the plight of the Cambodian people is something that was set in course because of America's foolish war in Vietnam. This is nothing more than an aftermath of that war. And it was a mistake for us to get into Vietnam, and the people of Cambodia are continuing to pay the price.

The fact is that we know that Hun Sen was actually ferried into Cambodia on the back of Vietnamese tanks during an upheaval in trying to get rid of Pol Pot, and this type of turmoil has been a horror story for this wonderful group of people in Cambodia who deserve much more than what they have had to experience.

Let me just say that American's greatest mistake, I think, was in 1993. I was there for that election, and the people actually voted against Hun Sen. And it was very clear that Hun Sen had lost the election. And our Ambassador at the time decided, oh, my goodness, they are threatening violence if we don't permit their—if we don't acquiesce to the demand that there be a sharing of power, and Hun Sen would be part of the sharing of power.

That decision, that one decision, has condemned the people of Cambodia to oppression and corruption never—we never imagined. The fact is, Hun Sen, yeah, he was power-sharing and he brutally, slowly but surely, eliminated all the rest of the people who were sharing power and eliminated the democratic process.

Today, what we need, and I am going to suggest this, I would like to hear about our witnesses, we should—we have a thing called the Magnitsky Act. Now, I happened to have voted—I think I voted for the Act, but I was against the name Magnitsky, because I didn't think that that had been proven in that case. However, the principle of the Magnitsky Act is exactly the right thing, and that is, let's find out the specific tyrants and criminals that are plaguing innocent people, like the people of Cambodia, and hold them specifically responsible. And try to find out where they bank—put their money, where is their bank accounts, and actually find ways of putting the law against them. I would like to have your opinion on how we might do that in Cambodia.

And, finally, let me just say this: If nothing else, today, we are telling the people of Cambodia, we are on your side. We are telling Hun Sen and his gang of criminals that now keep him in power, we are not on your side. We are on the side of the people of Cambodia and the side of a free and democratic Cambodia, and it is time for Hun Sen to go.

Mr. YOHO. Thank you for your comments.

We will next go to Mr. Chabot from Ohio.

Mr. CHABOT. Thank you, Mr. Chairman.

I happen—as Alan mentioned, I am co-chair of the Congressional Cambodian Caucus, and we have been working on this for quite some time. I want to thank him for his involvement there, Chairman Royce, and many others. And as Mr. Lowenthal mentioned, there is a resolution that we are submitting today, which essentially reaffirms the United States' commitment to democracy, human rights, and the rule of law in Cambodia.

That being said, although there were some bright spots awhile back with respect to Cambodia, I have to say that, under Hun Sen, we are about as far from a democracy as you can get. Shutting down independent press, suppressing opposition and civil society, threatening civil war if your party doesn't win, jailing your political opponent, and then dissolving their party so there is essentially no opposition, that is not a democracy. And so they are jeopardizing their relationship with the United States and the West. But they think, oh, that is okay because we have China on our side. And it is not surprising, because that is one of the other countries on this globe which has just about as much democracy as Cambodia does right now, which is zero.

And so if they want the human rights and the democracy of the PRC, that is what they are—that is what they are getting. And the Cambodian people deserve so much better than that, particularly when you consider the trauma that this nation has been through, where approximately a quarter of the population was wiped out under the Khmer Rouge.

And so, in any event, it is a terrible shame and travesty what is occurring in Cambodia right now, because it could be so much better. But this leader will not let the people of Cambodia decide who is going to control the country and who is going to rule the country and who—he wants it for himself. And it is just a shame. But, people of Cambodia, know that you have a lot of friends here in this country and all around the globe that are pulling for you and what is best for you. And so we hope that this hearing will draw some attention to that.

That being said, I also am the co-chair of the Congressional Turkish Caucus, and we had a meeting that started at 2 o'clock that I have to run to, but I will be back if we get finished there.

And, Alan, thank you for your hard work in this area.

I yield back.

Mr. YOHO. Thank you for your comments.

Does any other members have opening statements? Mr. Brooks?

Mr. BROOKS. No, sir. I am just waiting for the witnesses.

Mr. YOHO. All righty. And we are going to do that right now.

Ms. Oliva Enos, policy analyst at the Asian Studies Center at The Heritage Foundation. Thank you for being here. Ms. Mona Kem, daughter of the person that is in jail, your father—I can't imagine how hard this is for you to be here—deputy director-general of public affairs to the Cambodia National Rescue Party, and daughter of Kem Sokha, president of the Cambodia National Rescue Party. And Mr. Kenneth Wollack, president of the National Democratic Institute.

If you guys would—you have your timer up there. The green light is the beginning, it is 5 minutes. We will gently let you know when time comes up, and keep your remarks there. And then we look forward to getting your information so that we can help draft resolutions and direct policies for our government to, hopefully, bring this situation in Cambodia to an end.

So, with that, Ms. Enos, go ahead.

STATEMENT OF MS. OLIVIA ENOS, POLICY ANALYST, ASIAN STUDIES CENTER, DAVIS INSTITUTE FOR NATIONAL SECURITY AND FOREIGN POLICY, THE HERITAGE FOUNDATION

Ms. ENOS. Chairman Yoho, Ranking Member Sherman, and members of the subcommittee, thank you for the opportunity to testify before you this afternoon.

My name is Olivia Enos. I am a policy analyst in the Asian Studies Center at The Heritage Foundation. The views I express in this testimony are my own and should not be construed as representing any official position of The Heritage Foundation.

Cambodia's democracy is in peril. On September 2, Kem Sokha, president of the opposition Cambodia National Rescue Party, CNRP, was taken from his home, arrested, and indefinitely imprisoned on trumped up charges of treason. Kem Sokha's arrest triggered a downward spiral. Just a month later, on October 6, the Cambodian Interior Ministry filed a lawsuit to dissolve the opposition party. The CNRP was officialty dissolved by the Cambodian Supreme Court on November 16.

In just 3 months' time, Hun Sen, the leader of the ruling Cambodian People's Party, CPP, has eviscerated the CNRP, effectively crippling the only viable opposition to Hun Sen's 32-year reign, ahead of 2018 elections.

Since Kem Sokha's arrest, at least 100 CNRP parliamentarians and political leaders fled Cambodia. And the crackdown on civil society is severe. Shortly after Kem Sokha's arrest, Hun Sen proclaimed that he will rule for another 10 years.

The CPP's anemic electoral victory in 2013 was too slim for Hun Sen. In 2013, the opposition garnered 55 of the 123 seats in the assembly, leaving the ruling party with only 68 seats. Clearly, Hun Sen does not want to risk a potential opposition victory in 2018, which is why he has shut down the opposition long before it could become a viable threat to his three decades' long grip on power. Since the opposition was dissolved, the White House has stated that "on current course, next year's elections will not be legitimate, free, nor fair."

The U.S. Government response has gotten increasingly stronger. After releasing several statements, the Department of State took concrete action by pulling U.S. support for upcoming 2018 elections, and just last week, by restricting travel for individuals involved in undermining democracy in Cambodia.

Congress has taken similarly positive steps to hold the Cambodian Government to account. A bipartisan resolution introduced by Senators McCain, Durbin, and Rubio passed the Senate on November 17, and affirmed U.S. commitment to a democratic Cambodia, reiterated the value of the Paris Peace Agreements, and condemned the crackdown on civil society. The resolution also called for Treasury to consider placing all senior Cambodian officials implicated in the abuses on the Specially Designated Nationals list. Cambodia is at a crossroads, and the U.S. Government, in conjunction with the international community, should take action to hold Cambodian officials accountable.

In 1993, after the defeat of the Khmer Rouge, the U.S. and 18 other international signatories to the Paris Peace Agreement agreed to ensure the right to self-determination of the Cambodian people through free and fair elections. In this regard, signatories have a continuing moral obligation to assist Cambodia when the political process falters.

In my written submission, I offer several potential policy solutions to the current crises in Cambodia. Right now I will offer three.

First, the U.S. should consider sanctioning all individuals involved in undermining democracy in Cambodia under relevant Treasury Department authorities. Raising the financial risk to engaging in such behavior has the potential to deter future actions that erode democracy. Potential mechanisms could include invoking the Global Magnitsky Act, which allows individuals to be targeted on human rights and corruption grounds, or by placing individuals on this Specially Designated Nationals list, as was recommended by Senate Resolution 279.

Second, the U.S. Government should consider forming a Cambodia contact group comprised of key signatories to the Paris Peace Agreement. These signatories could include the U.S., Japan, Indonesia, Australia, the U.K., and France. Japan, in particular, has a critical role to play, but has thus far not done much in response to recent events in Cambodia. Given the severe deterioration in democracy there, the group should reassemble to provide accountability and develop plans to get Cambodia back on the path of political reform.

Third, and finally, the U.S. should continue to publicly and privately press for the release of Kem Sokha. The U.S., along with other partners, such as the European Union, should draw attention to threats to democracy in Cambodia. Calling for Kem Sokha's release is the surest way to do that. In particular, statements from high ranking officials, such as the Secretary of State or the Deputy Secretary of State, may deter Hun Sen from further degenerating democracy in Cambodia.

Thank you for your time and attention. I am now open for questions.

[The prepared statement of Ms. Enos follows:]

The **Heritage Foundation**

CONGRESSIONAL TESTIMONY

"Cambodia's Descent: Policies to Support Democracy and Human Rights"

Cambodia: A Democracy in Peril

Testimony before the
Subcommittee on Asia and the Pacific in the Committee on Foreign Affairs

United States House of Representatives

December 12, 2017

Olivia Enos
Policy Analyst, Asian Studies Center
The Heritage Foundation

My name is Olivia Enos. I am a policy analyst in the Asian Studies Center at The Heritage Foundation. The views I express in this testimony are my own and should not be construed as representing any official position of The Heritage Foundation.

Cambodia's democracy is in peril. On September 2nd, President of the opposition Cambodian National Rescue Party (CNRP), Kem Sokha, was taken from his home, arrested, and indefinitely imprisoned on trumped up charges of treason.[1] Kem Sokha's arrest triggered a downward spiral. Just a month later on October 6th, the Cambodian Interior Ministry filed a lawsuit to dissolve the opposition party, claiming that the opposition colluded with the U.S. government to overthrow the current Cambodian leadership.[2] The CNRP was official dissolved by the Cambodian Supreme Court on November 16th.[3]

In just three months time, the leader of the ruling Cambodian People's Party (CPP), Hun Sen, has completely demobilized the CNRP—effectively crippling the only viable opposition to Hun Sen's 32-

---

[1]Olivia Enos, "Kem Sokha's Arrest Yet Another Sign of Serious Backslides in Cambodian Democracy," *Forbes*, September 14, 2017, https://www.forbes.com/sites/oliviaenos/2017/09/14/kem-sokhas-arrest-yet-another-sign-of-serious-backslides-in-cambodian-democracy/#4cc5c7c5323c (accessed December 7, 2017).
[2]Prak Chan Thul, "Cambodian Government Files Lawsuit to Dissolve Main Opposition Party," Reuters, October 6, 2017, https://www.reuters.com/article/us-cambodia-politics/cambodian-government-files-lawsuit-to-dissolve-main-opposition-party-idUSKBN1CB0U1 (accessed December 7, 2017).
[3]Julia Wallace, "Cambodia's Top Court Dissolves Main Opposition Party," *The New York Times*, November 16, 2017, https://www.nytimes.com/2017/11/16/world/asia/cambodia-court-opposition.html (accessed December 7, 2017).

year reign ahead of the expected July 2018 elections. Since Kem Sokha's arrest, at least 100 CNRP parliamentarians and political leaders fled Cambodia. Shortly after Kem Sokha's arrest, Hun Sen proclaimed that he will rule for another 10 years.[4]

The crackdown on civil society is severe. In the months prior to Kem Sokha's arrest, there were already signs that Hun Sen and his cadres were attempting to silence alternative voices. After the release of a CNN documentary on sex trafficking in Cambodia in July, the Cambodian government targeted Agape International Missions (AIM), an anti-trafficking nongovernmental organization (NGO) featured in the documentary for its work fighting sex trafficking in Cambodia.[5] Hun Sen's decision to shut down AIM is reflective of a growing trend toward authoritarianism in Cambodia and should be viewed as a broader attempt at silencing civil society.[6] Around the same time, the Cambodian government issued a letter ordering election-monitoring NGO's to cease their activities.[7] This action was followed up with the expulsion of the National Democratic Institute (NDI) and all foreign staff members whom the Cambodian government accused of tax evasion and colluding with the opposition to overthrow the ruling party.[8] This is in spite of the fact that NDI worked with both the CNRP and the CPP to provide political party training and other forms of democracy assistance.[9] The Cambodia Daily, the main English language newspaper in Cambodia, was shut down due to allegations of tax evasion levied by the Cambodian government.[10] Radio stations are under threat, too, with Radio Free Asia forced to suspend it's in-country operations.[11] This is nothing short of an onslaught against free speech and freedom of the press. It is a clear attempt to silence opposing voices and limit transparency ahead of 2018 elections.

Hun Sen is taking a page out of the 2013 elections playbook. In the lead-up to the 2013 elections, former opposition leader Sam Rainsy was in self-imposed exile due to baseless charges leveled against

---

[4]The Editorial Board, "Cambodia's Democracy Betrayed," *The New York Times*, September 11, 2017, https://www.nytimes.com/2017/09/11/opinion/cambodia-democracy-hun-sen.html (accessed December 7, 2017).

[5]Alexandra Field, Dan Tham, and Mark Tutton, "Life after trafficking: The Girls Sold for Sex by Their Mothers," CNN, September 6, 2017, http://www.cnn.com/2017/07/24/asia/return-to-cambodia-sex-trafficking/index.html (accessed December 7, 2017).

[6]Olivia Enos, "Recent Removal of Anti-Trafficking Organization Bad Sign for Civil Society in Cambodia," Providence, August 4, 2017, https://providencemag.com/2017/08/recent-removal-anti-trafficking-organization-bad-sign-civil-society-cambodia-agape-international-missions/ (accessed December 7, 2017).

[7]Human Rights Watch, "Cambodia: Revoke Ban on Election Monitors", July 9, 2017, https://www.hrw.org/news/2017/07/09/cambodia-revoke-ban-election-monitors (accessed October 13, 2017).

[8]Ananth Baliga, "Breaking: NDI to Be Shuttered, Foreign Staff Expelled," *The Phnom Penh Post*, August 23, 2017, http://www.phnompenhpost.com/national/breaking-ndi-be-shuttered-foreign-staff-expelled (accessed December 7, 2017), and Hannah Beech, "Cambodia Orders Expulsion of Foreign Staff Members With American Nonprofit," *The New York Times*, August 23, 2017, https://www.nytimes.com/2017/08/23/world/asia/cambodia-us-ngo-hun-sen-nonprofit-crackdown.html (accessed December 7, 2017).

[9]NDI, "Statement on Cambodian Government's Decision to Shut Down NDI's Office in Cambodia," August 23, 2017, https://www.ndi.org/publications/statement-cambodian-government%E2%80%99s-decision-shut-down-ndis-office-cambodia (accessed December 7, 2017).

[10]Thomas Beller, "The Devastating Shutdown of the Cambodia Daily," *The New Yorker*, September 12, 2017, https://www.newyorker.com/news/news-desk/the-devastating-shutdown-of-the-cambodia-daily (accessed December 7, 2017).

[11]BBG, "Statement from Radio Free Asia's President on Cambodia," September 12, 2017, https://www.bbg.gov/2017/09/12/statement-radio-free-asias-president-cambodia/ (accessed December 7, 2017).

him by the Cambodian government.[12] In the final hour, he was permitted to return to Cambodia, but just late enough that he could not run as the main opposition presidential candidate.[13] This did not stop the opposition from garnering 55 of the 123 seats in the assembly, leaving the ruling party with 68 seats.[14] This modest electoral victory was too slim for Hun Sen and too close to an electoral victory for the opposition for comfort. This was in spite of the fact that Hun Sen kept journalists on a tight leash, instituted restrictions on local radio stations, banned foreign broadcasting, and limited the capabilities of Radio Free Asia and Voice of America, and has long controlled many television stations.[15]

While the 2013 election was mostly free of violence,[16] it is questionable whether it met the standard of "free and fair." An estimated 20,000 national and international observers were present throughout the elections, including U.S.-based organizations, Transparency International, and the International Republican Institute.[17] Many of them expressed concern about the process and accuracy of the outcome. Some observers claim that as many as 10,000 voting irregularities occurred during the 2013 elections.[18] Major issues include an estimated 10 percent of the population who were unable to find their names on the voting registry, indelible ink easily removed from fingers after voting, and an unusually large number of temporary voting cards distributed in the weeks and months leading up to the elections.[19] The Committee for Free and Fair Election in Cambodia (COMFREL) noted that not only were election irregularities significantly higher than during the last assembly elections in 2008, but COMFREL was particularly concerned with the number of temporary voting cards issued. According to COMFREL's records, 1 million people received temporary voting cards for the 2012 commune elections and an additional 700,000 people received them for the 2013 elections.[20] Such

---

[12]Prak Chan Thul, "Cambodian Opposition Leader Rainsy Pardoned Ahead of Election," Reuters, July 12, 2013, https://www.reuters.com/article/us-cambodia-election-rainsy/cambodian-opposition-leader-rainsy-pardoned-ahead-of-election-idUSBRE96B0BX20130712 (accessed December 7, 2017).

[13]RFA, "Sam Rainsy Claims His Party Won Enough Seats to Form Government," July 30, 2013, http://www.rfa.org/english/news/cambodia/election-07302013190248.html (accessed December 7, 2017).

[14]Walter Lohman and Olivia Enos, "Promoting True Democratic Transition in Cambodia," Heritage Foundation *Backgrounder* No. 2898, March 31, 2014, http://www.heritage.org/asia/report/promoting-true-democratic-transition-cambodia.

[15]Reporters Without Borders, "Local Media Still Censored in Run-up to General Elections," July 26, 2013, http://en.rsf.org/cambodia-local-media-still-censored-in-run-26-07-2013,44982.html (accessed December 7, 2017); news release, "Cambodia: Respect Freedom of Expression as Elections Approach," Freedom House, July 21, 2013, http://www.freedomhouse.org/sites/default/files/Cambodia%20-%20Joint%20Public%20Statement%20-%20Freedom%20of%20Expression%20-%207%20-%2021-%2013.pdf (accessed December 7, 2017); and Associated Press, "Cambodia Reverses Ban on Foreign Radio Programs," June 30, 2013, http://www.cbc.ca/news/world/cambodia-reverses-ban-on-foreign-radio-programs-1.1385916 (accessed December 7. 2017).

[16]"Cambodian Forces Clash with Opposition Amid Post-Election Deadlock; 1 Dead, 7 Wounded," *The Washington Post*, September 14, 2014, http://www.washingtonpost.com/world/asia_pacific/cambodia-opposition-pressures-government-with-new-rally-amid-post-election-deadlock/2013/09/14/93da1428-1db2-11e3-80ac-96205cacb45a_story.html (accessed September 24, 2013).

[17]International Republican Institute, "Cambodia Pre-Election Watch," July 28, 2013.

[18]Kuch Naren, "Election Was Not Free or Fair, Coalition of 21 NGOs Says," *The Cambodia Daily*, September 7, 2013, http://www.cambodiadaily.com/elections/election-was-not-free-or-fair-coalition-of-21-ngos-says-41839/ (accessed December 7, 2017).

[19]Transparency International, "Final Election Observation Report on Cambodia's 2013 National Election," September 2013, http://ticambodia.org/library/wp-content/files_mf/1438020883TICsReporton2013NationalElection.pdf (accessed December 7, 2017).

[20]Colin Meyn, "Comfrel Reports Spike in Election Irregularities," *The Cambodia Daily*, August 16, 2013, http://www.cambodiadaily.com/elections/comfrel-reports-spike-in-election-irregularities-39918/ (accessed December 7, 2017).

large numbers of people purportedly losing their permanent voter registration are implausible and call into question whether fraud took place.

In response to concerns about the legitimacy of the elections, the opposition carried out a series of largely peaceful protests, including an opposition boycott of the parliament, between July 2013 and July 2014. Protests and the boycott ended after the CPP offered a deal to the CNRP. It did not meet all of the previous stipulations outlined by the opposition, but the compromise prioritized reform to the National Election Committee (NEC)—presumably to make it a more objective adjudicator of future election results. Previously, all eleven NEC members were pro-CPP. Reforms required that nine members sit on the NEC: Four are CPP, four are CNRP, and one member will be a mutually agreed upon mediator.[21] The CPP also released seven recently arrested members of the opposition and cleaned up the nation's voting records. While the Cambodian government followed through with NEC reform, the person who held the position as unbiased mediator—a representative of the Cambodian NGO community—was later jailed.[22]

Clearly, Hun Sen does not want to risk a potential opposition victory in 2018, which is why he has shut down the opposition long before it could become a viable threat to his three-decades-long grip on power. The Cambodian government's decision to dissolve the opposition makes the impossibility of holding free and fair elections a foregone conclusion. The White House issued a statement reiterating this sentiment, saying, "On current course next year's election will not be legitimate, free or fair."[23]

The initial U.S. government response to Kem Sokha's arrest was modest at best. The State Department issued a limited statement condemning the arrest of Kem Sokha and highlighting backsliding trends in democracy in Cambodia on September 3.[24] The U.S. Embassy in Phnom Penh made a more forward-leaning statement similarly condemning Kem Sokha's arrest on September 12.[25] The embassy's statement focused principally on countering the accusation by the Cambodian government that Kem Sokha colluded with the U.S. government to undermine the government of Cambodia. During President Trump's visit to Asia, Deputy Assistant to the President and Senior Director for Asian Affairs Matt Pottinger and Deputy Assistant Secretary of State for Southeast Asia W. Patrick Murphy, in their meeting with Cambodian Foreign Minister Prak Sokhonn on November 14th, expressed concerns regarding backslides in democracy and highlighted the detention of Kem Sokha.[26]

---

[21]Olivia Enos, "Cambodia: Deal Doesn't End Need to Remain Vigilant," The Daily Signal, July 24, 2014, http://dailysignal.com/2014/07/24/cambodia-deal-doesnt-end-need-remain-vigilant/ (accessed December 7, 2017).
[22]Human Rights Watch, "Cambodia: Free 'ADHOC Five' Rights Defenders," December 1, 2016, https://www.hrw.org/news/2016/12/01/cambodia-free-adhoc-five-rights-defenders (accessed December 7, 2017).
[23]The White House, "Statement by the Press Secretary on Setbacks to Democracy in Cambodia," November 16, 2017, https://www.whitehouse.gov/the-press-office/2017/11/16/statement-press-secretary-setbacks-democracy-cambodia (accessed December 7, 2017).
[24]News release, "Arrest of Cambodian Opposition Leader," U.S. Department of State, September 3, 2017, https://www.state.gov/r/pa/prs/ps/2017/09/273808.htm (accessed December 7, 2017).
[25]U.S. Embassy in Cambodia, "Opening Statement by Ambassador William A. Heidt at a Press Availability," September 12, 2017, https://kh.usembassy.gov/opening-statement-ambassador-william-heidt-press-availability/(accessed December 7, 2017).
[26]U.S. Mission to ASEAN, "Press Release, November 14, 2017," November 14, 2017, https://asean.usmission.gov/press-release-november-14-2017/ (accessed December 7, 2017).

After the dissolution of the CNRP just two days later, the White House issued a stronger statement saying, "It is becoming increasingly evident to the world that the Cambodian government's restrictions on civil society, suppression of the press, and banning of more than 100 opposition leaders from political activities have significantly set back Cambodia's democratic development and placed its economic growth and international standing at risk."[27] In the statement, the U.S. announced its decision to cut funding for the Cambodian National Election Committee and its administration ahead of the 2018 election. In other words, the U.S. government pulled its support for next year's elections. It also repeated calls to release Kem Sokha and to allow the CNRP to continue with its usual political activities. This was a positive step that communicated that there are repercussions to Hun Sen and his cronies if they continue to undermine democratic institutions in the country.

On December 6th, the State Department restricted travel for "individuals involved in undermining democracy in Cambodia."[28] The statement accompanying the visa ban suggested that there might be additional follow-on actions if conditions worsen. It also communicated that the visa ban could be rolled back if conditions, such as recognizing the CNRP as the legitimate opposition and releasing Kem Sokha, are met. The Cambodian government has repeatedly communicated that it did not believe that the U.S. would institute sanctions or a visa ban, so this action, as well as future action should make clear that their will be no impunity for persons who erode democracy.

Congress has similarly taken positive steps to hold the Cambodian government to account. A resolution introduced by Senators John McCain (R–AZ), Dick Durbin (D–IL), and Marco Rubio (R–FL) passed the Senate on November 17th. The resolution affirmed U.S. commitment to a democratic Cambodia, reiterated the value of the Paris Peace Agreements (to which the U.S. is a signatory and agreed to hold Cambodia accountable for backslides in democracy and human rights), and condemned the uptick in cracking down on civil society, among other things.[29] The resolution also called for the release of Kem Sokha, electoral reform, and for Treasury to "consider placing all senior Cambodian government officials implicated in the abuses noted above on the Specially Designated Nationals List (SDN)."[30]

Congress is also currently reviewing the State, Foreign Operations, and Related Programs bill that sets appropriations for 2018 U.S. foreign assistance, including to Cambodia. At present, the House and Senate are reconciling their respective versions of the bill. The House version conditions 25 percent of international security assistance to Cambodia on the country's willingness to "cease efforts to intimidate civil society and the political opposition in Cambodia" and its support for the

---

[27]The White House, "Statement by the Press Secretary on Setbacks to Democracy in Cambodia," November 16, 2017, https://www.whitehouse.gov/the-press-office/2017/11/16/statement-press-secretary-setbacks-democracy-cambodia (accessed December 7, 2017).
[28]U.S. Department of State, "Visa Restrictions on Individuals Responsible for Undermining Cambodian Democracy," December 6, 2017, https://www.state.gov/r/pa/prs/ps/2017/12/276288.htm#.Wig9ip5FpCE.twitter (accessed December 7, 2017).
[29]U.S. Congress, "Reaffirming the Commitment of the United States to Promote Democracy, Human Rights, and the Rule of Law in Cambodia," S. RES. 279, November 16, 2017, https://www.congress.gov/115/bills/sres279/BILLS-115sres279ats.pdf (accessed December 7, 2017).
[30]Ibid.

"conduct of free and fair elections," among other conditions.[31] The Senate version of the bill conditions all assistance to the central government in the bill on Cambodia's commitment to democracy. It also goes farther by including the "release of jailed opposition leaders and civil society activists" among the conditions and by imposing a visa ban on Cambodian officials known to undermine democracy in Cambodia.[32] If the bill passes, the law will send a clear signal to Hun Sen and his CPP party cadres that the U.S. is serious about its commitment to holding the Cambodian government to account for undermining democracy.

Cambodia's 2013 elections were a turning point in its democratic development. It has become clear that public support for Hun Sen's leadership has detioriated to the point that it threatens his continued hold on office. Some attribute this shift in the electoral support to shifting demographics in Cambodia; as the younger generation comes of voting age, many were not alive during the genocide committed by the Khmer Rouge and are therefore less responsive to Hun Sen's scare tactics.[33] The fact that the opposition nearly won the election made it a watershed moment.

Now, Cambodia is at yet another crossroads—but this one is far more sinister than the last.

The role of the U.S. in Cambodia has been and always will be to serve as an accountability partner that steers Cambodia back on the path toward political reform. After the Khmer Rouge terror and Vietnamese invasion, the international community oversaw a democratic transition in Cambodia.[34] To end the conflict and promote a free Cambodia, on October 23, 1991, the U.S. and 18 other international signatories to the Paris Peace Agreement assented to "promote and encourage respect for and observance of human rights and fundamental freedoms in Cambodia."[35] The agreement also ensured the "the right to self-determination of the Cambodian people through free and fair elections."[36] In this regard, signatories have a continuing obligation to assist Cambodia when the political process falters, as it so visibly is today.

Representative Alan Lowenthal (D–CA) aptly noted that it is not for the U.S. to decide who will be the electoral victor in Cambodia. The outcome of elections is most evidently for the Cambodian people to determine. The U.S., as a global purveyor of freedom and human rights worldwide, has a strong interest in seeing freedom restored in Cambodia.

---

[31]Harold Rogers, "Making Appropriations for the Department of State, Foreign Operations, and Related Programs for the Fiscal Year Ending September 30, 2018, and for Other Purposes," H.R. Report No. 115, p. 180, https://appropriations.house.gov/uploadedfiles/fy18-sfops-sub xml.pdf (accessed December 7, 2017).
[32]Lindsey Graham, "Making Appropriations for the Department of State, Foreign Operations, and Related Programs for the Fiscal Year Ending September 30, 2018, and for Other Purposes," S. 1780 Report No. 115-152, p. 224, https://www.congress.gov/115/bills/s1780/BILLS-115s1780pcs.pdf (accessed December 7, 2017).
[33]Lohman and Enos, "Promoting True Democratic Transition in Cambodia."
[34]Asian Human Rights Commission, "Press Law," http://test.ahrchk.net/countries/cambodia/cambodian-laws/press law/press (accessed March 7, 2014).
[35]University of Notre Dame Kroc Institute for International Peace Studies, "Human Rights: Framework for a Comprehensive Political Settlement of the Cambodia Conflict," https://peaceaccords.nd.edu/provision/human-rights-framework-comprehensive-political-settlement-cambodia-conflict (accessed December 7, 2017).
[36]United Nations Transitional Authority in Cambodia, "Agreements on a Comprehensive Political Settlement of the Cambodia Conflict,"
1991, http://www.usip.org/sites/default/files/file/resources/collections/peace agreements/agree comppol 10 231991.pdf (accessed December 7, 2017).

The need for the U.S. to take action in the short-term is critical. The U.S. role in getting Cambodia back on the path toward democracy includes:

- **Sanctioning all individuals involved in undermining democracy in Cambodia under relevant Treasury Department authorities.** The State Department's recent decision to institute a visa ban against Cambodian officials undermining democracy was a positive first step that should be followed up by additional efforts to hold Hun Sen and the CPP financially responsible for their abuse of power. Raising the financial risk to engaging in such behavior has the potential to deter future actions that erode democracy. Potential mechanisms could include invoking Global Magnitsky authorities, which allow individuals to be targeted on both human rights and corruption grounds or placing individuals on the SDN list as was recommended by S. Res 279. Either way, Hun Sen and CPP members need to know that the U.S. will hold Cambodian individuals responsible for their role in undermining the political reform process.
- **Continuing to publicly and privately press for the release of Kem Sokha.** Hun Sen and the CPP have a history of targeting opposition leadership as a ploy to undermine free and fair elections. The U.S., along with other partners in Europe and elsewhere, should draw attention to threats to democracy in Cambodia. Calling for Kem Sokha's release is the easiest way to do that. In particular, statements from high-ranking officials, such as the Secretary of State or Deputy Secretary of State, may impact Hun Sen's decision-making calculus and would signal that the U.S. is watching the degenerating conditions in Cambodia closely.
- **Publicly endorsing the language of the State, Foreign Operations, and Related Programs bill by the Trump Administration—particularly the tougher Senate language—conditioning assistance to Cambodia.** It should especially support the provision that places broader-sweeping conditions on U.S. aid to Cambodia. The Administration should also endorse the language of S. Res 279 which calls for Cambodian officials to be placed on the SDN list.
- **Pressing the Hun Sen government to grant access to outside election monitors ahead of 2018 elections.** In spite of the U.S. government's recent decision to pull funding for the NEC and the 2018 elections, it is critical that election monitors be permitted to oversee the 2018 election to determine the extent of the damage to political and electoral institutions. It is equally critical to get a pulse on trends in the electorate and changes in public opinion ahead of the election. While the free and fair nature of the election is already a foregone conclusion if the Hun Sen government sticks to its guns and upholds the Cambodian Supreme Court's decision to dissolve the opposition, the functionality of other institutions should be monitored and evaluated. Election monitors, such as the National Democratic Institute, the International Republic Institute, and the National Endowment for Democracy, can monitor the election process even without government support. U.S.-led and internationally led election monitors should have access to Cambodia prior to, during, and after the 2018 election cycle.

Threats to democracy in Cambodia precede the most recent crisis and point to broader, systemic threats to freedom in Cambodia.

The U.S. should seek to craft a more comprehensive, long-term strategy by:

- **Forming a Cambodia Contact Group comprised of key signatories to the Paris Peace Agreement.** Signatories already have an obligation to hold Cambodia to account in order to ensure that human rights are respected and that free and fair elections are held. Key signatories could include the Australia, France, Indonesia, Japan, the U.K., and the U.S. Japan, in particular, has a critical role to play, but has thus far not done much in response to recent events in Cambodia. The U.S. should, at a minimum, seek greater cooperation from Japanese counterparts. Given the severe deterioration in democracy in Cambodia, the group should re-assemble to provide accountability and develop plans to get Cambodia back on the path of political reform.

- **Pressing for the release of political prisoners in Cambodia.** As of June 2017, there were at least 20 individuals detained as political prisoners in Cambodia.[37] That number does not include Kem Sokha, who was detained last month, or other CNRP parliamentarians detained since the most recent crackdown. Deputy president of the CNRP, Mu Sochua, says that she felt her freedom was unprecedentedly compromised, which led her to flee the country.[38] Hun Sen continues to issue threats to opposition parliamentarians. In the coming months, the U.S. should watch closely to see if more individuals are taken as political prisoners.
- **Conducting a review of its democracy programming and economic assistance to Cambodia.** Given the lack of sufficient progress in many areas of Cambodia's democracy since 1993, the U.S. Agency for International Development should conduct a formal review of its democracy programming to identify deficiencies in current areas of focus and identify new areas and mechanisms for political development. As scholar Dr. Sophal Ear demonstrates in his 2012 book, *AID Dependence in Cambodia: How Foreign Assistance Undermines Democracy*, foreign assistance has weakened political accountability in Cambodia. Congress and the Administration should be prepared to make changes to Cambodia's aid packages in response to current conditions and the results of reviews of the programming.

It is in the U.S. interest for Cambodia to be free and prosperous. Silence in the face of deteriorating conditions in Cambodia may mean the end of political reform in Cambodia. The U.S. should take swift action to guide Cambodia back to a path of freedom and democracy.

---

[37] Cambodia's Political Prisoners, "Political Prisoner Count: 20 (as of June 2017)," https://www.licadho-cambodia.org/political_prisoners/ (accessed December 7, 2017).

[38] Holly Robertson, "Cambodia, a Nominal Democracy, Lurches Toward Full-Blown Dictatorship," *Los Angeles Times*, October 10, 2017, http://www.latimes.com/world/asia/la-fg-cambodia-dictatorship-2017-story.html (accessed December 7, 2017).

* * * * * * * * * * * * * * * * * *

The Heritage Foundation is a public policy, research, and educational organization recognized as exempt under section 501(c)(3) of the Internal Revenue Code. It is privately supported and receives no funds from any government at any level, nor does it perform any government or other contract work.

The Heritage Foundation is the most broadly supported think tank in the United States. During 2016, it had hundreds of thousands of individual, foundation, and corporate supporters representing every state in the U.S. Its 2016 income came from the following sources:

Individuals 75.3%
Foundations 20.3%
Corporations 1.8%
Program revenue and other income 2.6%

The top five corporate givers provided The Heritage Foundation with 1.0% of its 2016 income. The Heritage Foundation's books are audited annually by the national accounting firm of RSM US, LLP.

Mr. YOHO. Thank you for your comments there.

And now we will go to Ms. Kem.

And, you know, I know this has got to be a hard thing, you know, talking about this in front of this committee with your father, Kem Sokha, incarcerated right now. So I would love to hear from you, and thank you for being here.

STATEMENT OF MS. MONOVITHYA KEM, DEPUTY DIRECTOR-GENERAL OF PUBLIC AFFAIRS, CAMBODIA NATIONAL RESCUE PARTY (DAUGHTER OF KEM SOHKA, PRESIDENT, CAMBODIA NATIONAL RESCUE PARTY)

Ms. KEM. Chairman Yoho, Ranking Member Sherman, and members of the subcommittee, thank you so much for this opportunity to testify today on the fragile state of Cambodia's democracy and the important role that the U.S. can play to protect the political rights of the Cambodian people in the lead up of our national election, which is scheduled for July 2018.

Twenty-six years after the signing of the Paris Peace Accord, Cambodia is once again facing a historic crossroads, which two options present. One, restoring democracy or dissenting into downright dictatorship.

The fundamental elements of the Paris Peace Accords have been violated by the ruling elites, and some of those violations—recent violation include, number one, the November 16 dissolution of the main opposition party, the CNRP, and the theft and redistribution of our seats, 55 seats in the national assembly to unelected smaller parties.

Number two, the unconstitutional and midnight arrest of the opposition leader, Kem Sokha, my father, without warrant, by heavily armed police raided into his house after midnight. That violated his parliamentary immunity. That echoed the terrifying tactics and divisive rhetoric of Cambodia's darkest past, the Khmer Rouge.

And, number three, the banning of 118 CNRP leaders from participating in politics, and the removal of about 5,000 of our commune councillors who were just elected earlier this year in June.

And, number four, the crackdown on independent media and civil society. Most brutally, the broad daylight assassination of the political analyst, Dr. Kem Ley.

Democracy and freedom are American values that echo universal ideals. I believe your country bedrock values resonate well with the Cambodian people's desire for change that is felt by all Cambodians of all walks of life. And it is not only the moral responsibility of the U.S. to protect democracy and human rights in Cambodia, I believe it is also in the U.S. interest.

The U.S. benefits by staying engaged in Asia to uphold the international rule-based order that underpins the global commerce and international security. So it is both in your interest and in protecting your values. The U.S. has already sent a clear signal, I believe, to the Cambodian Government in holding them responsible for the regression.

I want to thank both Houses of Congress. I want to thank the White House, the State Department, especially for the banning of— the visa ban that was placed last week, and also the continuous call for the release of Kem Sokha, without condition, and of other political prisoners, for free and fair election in 2018.

But it is important now that the U.S. place and force a deadline. It is very important to place a deadline with the Cambodian Government. If the Cambodian Government does not reverse course on time, as soon as possible, I believe further action needs to be taken by the U.S. And that include, number one, placing individual targeted sanctions on Cambodian Government officials that have been identified as undermining democracy through the global Magnitsky Act, or on the SDN list, as recommended by the Senate.

Number two, suspending any and all assistance that go directly to central Cambodian Government, including security-related assistance, as proposed by the Senate, State, and Appropriation Operation bill.

Number three, continue to provide democracy assistance to civil society, especially the NGOs that work on election-related matters.

Number four, reviewing Cambodia's eligibility for the generalized system of preferences, and sending a notice of that review as soon as possible to the Cambodian Government so that they have incentive to backtrack.

Number five, coordinating with like-minded countries and entities, such as Japan, the EU, Australia, and South Korea, to use their leverages in calling for the Cambodian Government to reverse course.

And, finally, number six, convening key signatories of the Paris Peace Accord to organize a synchronized global response to the Cambodian Government, because they have been attacking all the elements of the Paris Peace Accord.

The current oppression, I believe, if continued to—if allowed to continue, will generate political instability, because oppressed dissent tends to boil over, and then eventually that will lead to economic instability as well.

So I urge you to remain resolute in your call for the release of Kem Sokha and other political prisoners, for free and fair election in 2018 in Cambodia. And I believe Cambodia is worth your attention and action, because this crossroad actually presents an unprecedented opportunity that the country has not seen for decades. Big changes can happen, and we are an inch away from it.

Democracy is very much possible and it can happen very soon, and the U.S. can play a big role in helping Cambodia, telling an inspiring story to the world, that democracy can persist. Thank you.

[The prepared statement of Ms. Kem follows:]

Cambodia's Descent: Policies to Support Democracy and Human Rights"

Testimony before the
Subcommittee on Asia and the Pacific in the Committee on Foreign Affairs

United States House of Representatives

December 12th, 2017

Monovithya Kem

Member of Permanent Committee

Deputy Director-General of Public Affairs

The Cambodia National Rescue Party

Chairman Yoho, Ranking Member Sherman, and distinguished members of the subcommittee,

Thank you for the invitation to testify today about the fragile state of Cambodia's democracy and the vital role the United States can play to protect the political rights of the Cambodian people in the lead up to our national elections scheduled for July 2018. I am a member of the permanent committee of the Cambodia National Rescue Party (CNRP), the main democratic opposition party, which was recently, and unconstitutionally, dissolved. I am honored to appear before you today to offer an account of the Cambodian government's recent violations of the Paris Peace Accords, and their impacts on multiparty democracy, and to recommend a way forward to resurrect the spirit of the Accords and restore democratic stability and peace to Cambodia.

Let me begin by making clear that my concerns are about more than the opposition party or my father the opposition leader Kem Sokha, who has been a political prisoner for 103 days. My concern is for the livelihood of sixteen million people, the majority of whom are under the age of 35 and are hungry to take charge of their own destiny. My concern is about the struggle for free and fair elections in 2018 and for the Cambodian people to finally shape their own destiny free from the bonds of repression.

What is going wrong?

Twenty-six years after the world came together and negotiated the Paris Peace Accords to help Cambodia rebuild itself from the devastation caused by the Khmer Rouge and decades of civil strife, Cambodia once again faces an historic crossroads, where two options appear: either descent into outright dictatorship or a restoration of democracy.

Today, fundamental elements of the Accords have been violated by the Cambodian ruling elites through the systematic abuse of state institutions, including the courts, the executive, the army, the National Assembly, and even the anti-corruption body, just to name a few. By signing the Accords, Cambodia and the other signatories promised, and are obliged to strictly maintain and preserve national unity, sovereignty, territorial integrity and independence, as well as "ensure respect for and observance of human rights and fundamental freedoms" and "adhere to relevant international human rights instruments." As evidenced by recent developments, the Cambodian government has violated the core principles of the Accords through actions that undermine the Cambodian Constitution and the universal human rights and democratic freedoms of Cambodia's people. Examples of these violations and abuses include:

1. The November 16th dissolution of the Cambodia National Rescue Party (CNRP), the only opposition party elected to the National Assembly. The supreme court's groundless decision to dissolve CNRP directly violates the Cambodian Constitution, which states that Cambodia shall be ruled according "to the principles of liberal democracy and pluralism," and constituted impermissible discrimination based on political opinion in violation of Article 26 of the International Convention on Civil and Political Rights (ICCPR). The court's decision was made by judges who hold high-ranking leadership positions in the ruling party, further proving the biases of a court system repeatedly used by the ruling party to eliminate opposition and turn Cambodia into an effective one-party state. Furthermore, the theft and redistribution of the CNRP's 55 seats in the National Assembly to unelected minor parties in an effort to preserve a veneer of multiparty democracy also violated the Constitution, which states that Members of the National Assembly shall be chosen in a free and fair election. The Constitution never allows any institution to select legislators on behalf of the Cambodian voters, who are the sole bearers of this fundamental political right.

2. The illegal and unconstitutional arrest of the opposition leader Kem Sokha. In violation of his parliamentary immunity, Kem Sokha was arrested after midnight September 3rd, by police officers acting without a warrant. Cambodian law prohibits both warrantless arrests and arrests after 6 p.m. The act of breaking into his house after midnight was designed to terrorize. Like the dissolution of the CNRP, the arrest was a severe violation of a number of principles of the Paris Peace Accords, first, as a clear attempt by the ruling party to eliminate its only viable opposition by immobilizing the leader of a party that represents nearly half of the country in parliament and earned three million votes in the last election. In doing so, the Cambodian government has taken on millions of Cambodians as its enemies and effectively destroyed national unity, which it pledged in the Accords to preserve. Second, Kem Sokha was arrested for "treason," an all-too-familiar term that echoes the divisive rhetoric of Cambodia's darkest age. In the Paris Peace Accords, Cambodia has pledged "to take effective measures to ensure that the policies and practices of the past shall never be allowed to return." Treason was a widely used accusation by the Khmer Rouge to eliminate anyone it saw as a threat to its brutal regime. Arresting someone at night for being a "traitor" is the policy and practice of Cambodia's ugliest past that shall never be allowed to return—but sadly it has.

3. The ban of 118 CNRP leaders from participating in politics and the removal of roughly 5000 CNRP commune councilors who were just elected in June this year, bringing a balance of power to local government for the first time. These violations of universal political rights and fundamental freedoms show that the Cambodian government has been willing to disregard elections and sweep aside the will of the people. The Cambodian government took away the rights of these voters and political leaders to participate freely in politics.

4. The crackdown on the independent media and civil society, particularly the assassination of prominent political analyst Kem Ley. The Cambodian government has shut down critical newspapers, radio stations and non-governmental organizations that are key to establishing conditions for a free and fair election. The intent behind the crackdown is very clear: to ensure that the Cambodian people will not have access to the information they need to make informed decisions in the 2018 election. Journalists and activists, including both CNRP members and nonpartisan defenders of human rights, most notably land rights activist Tep Vanny, were imprisoned without due process. The most violent and terrifying stage of this crackdown was the public assassination in broad daylight of independent political analyst Kem Ley.

Today, anyone not a member or supporter of the ruling party lives in fear that they may become a target of state repression. Foreign residents, union organizers, journalists, NGO workers and even social media users now find themselves relegated to an environment where the Cambodian government may come to their house, without notice or credible basis, and accuse them of attempting to overthrow the government. Suddenly, at least half of the country becomes a suspect. The ruling elites have labeled other members of society their enemies.

Why should the U.S. care?

In 1991, countries from around the world rightly decided that they could no longer turn their back on the people of Cambodia after the suffering brought by the Khmer Rouge and decades of civil strife. To its credit, the United States was among these countries. A peace agreement was reached and the four Cambodian parties as well as many signatory countries signed the Paris Peace Accords 1991, which effectively ended civil war and guaranteed a free and fair election in Cambodia.

As a signatory to the Accords, the United States has a legal and moral responsibility to ensure that Cambodia does not fall back into an outright dictatorship. In fact, the U.S. intent to support human rights and democracy in Cambodia has been clear not only through the signing of Paris Peace Accords but also through your heavy investment in the form of foreign assistance worth over $1.7 billion focused not only on developing the economy but also bolstering civil society's efforts to organize and advocate. Democracy and freedom are American values that echo universal ideals. These ideals have taken root in Cambodian society as Cambodian people increasingly find the courage to defend our dignity and speak our hearts. Your country's bedrock values align very well with the desire for change felt deeply by the Cambodian people of all walks of life.

There is also a strategic calculus at play. Cambodia is one of the places around the world where there is a clear overlap between American interests and values. It is not only a moral responsibility of the United States to support democracy and freedom in Cambodia, but it is also in the U.S. interest to do so from a strategic foreign policy standpoint. In Asia, democracies tend to be more stable, open and prosperous, and also more likely to uphold the rules-based international order which underpins global commerce and international security.

The current Cambodian government has become increasingly unfriendly to the United States and its allies, and as it has acted increasingly at odds with the unity in ASEAN. This is troubling for the U.S. role and regional security in Asia-Pacific. And the U.S. benefits by staying engaged in Asia, the most economically dynamic region in the world.

What can the U.S. do to help Cambodia reverse course?

The United States has done much already. I commend both houses of Congress, The White House, and the State Department for taking concrete steps to hold the Cambodian government accountable for its regression. These steps include:

- The statement issued by the Department of State on December 6th, announcing that the Secretary of State will restrict entry to the U.S. for those Cambodian government officials (and their families) who are undermining democracy in Cambodia and reiterating the call for the unconditional release of Kem Sokha and for free fair elections;

-The passage of bipartisan Senate Resolution 279 on November 17th, introduced by Senators John McCain (R–AZ), Dick Durbin (D–IL), and Marco Rubio (R–FL). The resolution called for the release of Kem Sokha, free and fair elections, and for the Department of the Treasury to consider placing senior Cambodian officials responsible for democracy and human rights abuses on the Specially Designated Nationals List (SDN);

- The statement from the White House on November 16th, announcing the U.S. decision to cut funding for Cambodia's upcoming elections and calling for the release of Kem Sokha;

-The statement from the U.S. Mission to ASEAN on November 14th, on the meeting between Cambodian Foreign Minister Prak Sokhonn and Deputy Assistant to the President and Senior Director for Asian Affairs at the National Security Council Matthew Pottinger and Deputy Assistant Secretary of State for Southeast Asia W. Patrick Murphy. The meeting highlighted concerns on Kem Sokha's continued detention and overall deterioration of democracy in Cambodia;

-The State, Foreign Operations, and Related Programs bill (S. 1780) introduced on September 7th, by the Senate Appropriations Committee. The bill conditions all assistance to the Cambodian central government on respect for human rights and democracy including the release of opposition leaders and civil society activists. The bill also calls for a visa ban to be placed on Cambodian government officials who undermine democracy.

With these actions, the U.S. has sent a clear signal to the Cambodian government that it remains resolute in its support for human rights and democracy in Cambodia. It is important now for the US to communicate to the Cambodian government on a deadline to reverse course or further sanctions will be imposed. If the Cambodian government does not quickly reverse course, I believe further U.S.

action is needed as follows:

-Placing targeted financial sanctions on Cambodian government officials identified as undermining democracy through the SDN list as recommended by the Senate (S Res. 279) and/or through the Global Magnitsky Act;

-Suspending any and all assistance for the central Cambodian Government, including security-related assistance, as proposed in the Senate State and Foreign Operations bill (S. 1780);

-Continuing democracy assistance programs for civil society, particularly those engaged in election-related matters;

-Reviewing Cambodia's eligibility for the Generalized System of Preferences (GSP). A notice of this review needs to be sent to the Cambodian government soonest possible to provide incentive for backtracking;

-Coordinating with like-minded countries and entities (starting with Japan, the European Union, Australia, and South Korea) to use their leverages in calling on Cambodian Government to reverse course;

-Convening key signatories of the Paris Peace Accords to review the violations by the Cambodian Government and recommend a synchronized global response to the Cambodian government's assault on the Accords.

What are the risks of keeping the status quo?

The current oppression, if allowed to continue, will generate political instability as repressed dissent boils over; this will eventually trigger economic instability that will take the country backwards. Left unchecked, the Cambodian ruling elite will lead Cambodia toward the wrong side of history simply to preserve its power. If the signatories to the Paris Peace Accords allow impunity, the Cambodian government will believe that it is free to act irresponsibly. The lack of effective responses from the free world will be read by the Cambodian government as a clear indication that it is not accountable to the community of democracies, and that international assistance and trade relationships are a one-way obligation, where the Cambodian government is entitled to foreign aid and investment but not obligated to fulfill any responsibility to defending its democratic stability and the rights and freedoms of its people. Eventually, the abuse will extend beyond domestic issues. The Cambodian government will soon become an irresponsible regional actor by detaching itself from international laws and building alignments based on the personal benefits of the ruling elites.

Toward that end, I urge you to remain resolute in your calls for the immediate release of Kem Sokha and other prisoners of conscience, the restoration of the CNRP and of the political rights of its members and supporters, the establishment of conditions for free and fair elections in 2018, including reinstating banned media and ending judicial and political harassment of civil society groups critical of the government.

Cambodia is worth your attention and concrete action, because this crossroads presents an unprecedented opportunity for positive changes that the country has not seen in decades. The results of the 2013 national elections, the months-long peaceful protests that followed, as well as the results of the 2017 local elections, all provide evidence that we are an inch away from historic changes. It is worth your attention because Cambodia is one of the places in the world where your action will likely yield positive results during this gloomy time our world faces today. Democracy is very much possible in Cambodia and it can happen very soon, the U.S. can play a unique role in helping Cambodia tell an inspiring story to the region and the world about the power of perseverance in the face of adversity.

Mr. YOHO. Well, we appreciate it and you coming here testifying. That gets that message out to the world, and we will help you with that.

Mr. Wollack, from—the president of the National Democratic Institute. Go ahead.

STATEMENT OF MR. KENNETH WOLLACK, PRESIDENT, NATIONAL DEMOCRATIC INSTITUTE

Mr. WOLLACK. Mr. Chairman, Ranking Member Sherman, thank you for this opportunity to testify before the subcommittee on developments in Cambodia.

I am honored to appear here with Mona Kem. She and her imprisoned father are courageous champions for democracy in Cambodia.

And let me summarize my written testimony with these comments.

As has already been said here, the recent action by the Cambodian Government and the ruling CPP to dissolve the opposition CNRP, effectively transformed the country into a one-party state. The arrest of Kem Sokha, the leader of the CNRP, on spurious charges, the banning of over 100 opposition leaders from political activities, the arrests of political activists, and the crackdown of independent news media and civil society, have isolated the country and put its further development in serious doubt.

These and previous actions by the Cambodian Government are a clear violation of the spirit and letter of the 1991 Paris Peace Agreement, which ended the nation's 12-year civil war. That agreement, which Mona referred to, was signed by 19 governments, including the United States and China, and required Cambodia to respect human rights and called for Cambodia to follow a system of liberal democracy on the basis of pluralism. And I would recommend strongly a rereading of the provisions of that important document.

When the 1991 Paris Peace Agreement was signed, Cambodia was emerging from decades of war, the genocidal Khmer Rouge regime, and the Vietnamese occupation. The country was economically devastated, and the institutions of governance weak or nonexistent. In some areas, much progress has been made, largely due to the hard work by thousands of Cambodians and international donors.

The U.S. has played a major role in the country's development, funding projects in the fields of agriculture, education, and public health, and strengthening the electoral system, rule of law, political parties, and civil society.

NDI has focused its efforts in Cambodia on developing governance and building a more democratic political party system. Since 1992, NDI has sponsored hundreds of community-level multiparty dialogs, offering villagers the opportunity to engage in local governance, sponsored election campaign debates, and assisted citizen organizations to monitor the elections. We have also carried out programs, and I emphasize here, with both the ruling and opposition parties alike, to participate in elections, monitor polling, develop greater opportunities for women and youth, and build more democratic party structures.

Since the transitional period began in 1991, the ruling CPP has dominated the political landscape, maintaining control of the police, the military, civil bureaucracy, and virtually all of local government. However, the Peace Accord spawned a large number of civil society groups, which were able to operate, at times, with a surprising amount of freedom. Political parties too have had some space in which to operate. Although the government used civil defamation suits, the party registration law, and the filing of criminal charges to keep the opposition off balance.

At the same time, Cambodia's political history since the Paris Peace Accords can be characterized as a period marked by three distinct coups. The first coup occurred when the results of the 1993 elections, conducted by the United Nations Transitional Authority in Cambodia, UNTAC, were in effect overturned by the CPP, as Mr. Rohrbacher pointed out.

The second occurred in 1997 when Hun Sen brutally and violently overthrew his coalition partner, FUNCINPEC, and forced the opposition into exile.

The third coup, of course, occurred this year when the government disbanded the CNRP, the only opposition party that could effectively challenge them. The opposition strength was clearly growing, as has been noted here. In the 2013 national elections, the CNRP made a strong showing, increasing their seats in Parliament by nearly 50 percent, while the CPP saw their representation decline by 25 percent.

In the elections' aftermath, the CPP-led government became increasingly repressive, stepping up actions against civil society and the political opposition. Its motivation was obvious. The CPP's own internal polling, leaked to the press, showed the ruling party facing stiff opposition in the upcoming local and national election. And I would suggest rereading some of the questions in that poll that are included in my written statements. They actually foreshadow the exact actions taken by the CPP.

Commune council elections were held last June, resulting in a strong showing for the CNRP, which won 44 percent of the total votes cast. On August 23, NDI received a notice from the government ordering it to close its office and withdraw its international staff from the country within 7 days. The Voice of America, the Radio Free Asia, were also shuttered, as were dozens of local broadcast stations which carried VOA and RFA programming. The Cambodia Daily, the Independent English Language newspaper that had been operating since 1963 was forced to close.

The government's actions are clearly designed to maintain, at any price, the ruling party in power. They also place Cambodia more firmly in China's orbit. While the Cambodian Government was widely condemned by the international community for its recent repressive measures, China was quick to offer support, ignoring the provisions of the Paris Peace Agreement to which it is a signatory.

I want to recognize the actions taken by the U.S. Government in terminating assistance to Cambodia's election commission, and imposing visa restrictions on those Cambodian officials responsible for undermining democracy. These actions are important because they demonstrate that concrete measures will be taken unless certain conditions are met.

Let me just summarize by recommending possible other actions that could be taken. Number one, the withdrawal of all but humanitarian aid to the Government of Cambodia.

Two, continued support of nongovernmental organizations within Cambodia.

Three, altering the terms of trade with Cambodia, the U.S.'s largest export market for Cambodian goods, receiving 25 percent of Cambodian exports. The EU is the next largest. This provides leverage for inducing positive change.

Four, increase international pressure and dialog. Following the 1997 coup, an informal diplomatic network known as the Friends of Cambodia Group, helped Hun Sen and the political opposition come to an agreement on conditions under which the exiles would return to Cambodia to participate in national elections the following year. The U.N. withheld recognition of the government at that time, and similar moves might help pave the way for new negotiations.

And, finally, supporting the return of exiled political leaders. The CNRP remains a legitimate political force within Cambodia. However, over 100 opposition leaders and elected officials are in exile. As in 1997, continued support should be provided to the exiled opposition to help them convene and to communicate with their supporters and the international community. Thank you very much.

[The prepared statement of Mr. Wollack follows:]

Statement by
Kenneth Wollack

President, National Democratic Institute

House Committee on Foreign Affairs
Subcommittee on Asia and the Pacific

December 12, 2017

Mr. Chairman, Ranking Member Sherman, thank you for this opportunity to testify before the Subcommittee on developments in Cambodia.

Recent actions by Cambodia's government to dissolve the opposition Cambodia National Rescue Party (CNRP), effectively transformed the country into a one-party state. The arrest of Kem Sokha, the leader of the CNRP on spurious charges, the banning of over 100 opposition leaders from political activities, the arrests of political activists, and the crackdown on independent news media and civil society have isolated the country and put its further democratic development in serious doubt. In addition, the ruling Cambodia People's Party (CPP) is systematically replacing local and national lawmakers affiliated with the opposition with those loyal to the ruling CPP.

These and previous actions by the Cambodian government should be seen as nothing less than a clear violation of the spirit and letter of the 1991 Paris Peace Agreement, which ended the nation's 12 year civil war. That agreement -- signed by 19 governments, including the United States and China -- required Cambodia to respect human rights as enshrined in principal international human rights instruments, and called for Cambodia to follow "a system of liberal democracy on the basis of pluralism." The accords also mandated "periodic and genuine elections...with a requirement that electoral procedures provide a full and fair opportunity to organize and participate in the electoral process." Cambodia's descent into autocracy also threatens to overturn the efforts of the international community, which has spent billions of dollars on Cambodia's democratic development -- as well as the tireless work of countless Cambodian citizens -- over the past 26 years.

When the 1991 Paris Peace Agreement was signed, Cambodia was emerging from decades of war, the genocidal Khmer Rouge regime and Vietnamese occupation. The country was economically devastated and the institutions of governance weak or non-existent. In some areas, much progress has been made, largely due to the commitment of international donors and efforts of the many thousands of Cambodians who have worked to secure the vision of the peace accords and a better future for their country. The U.S. has played a major role in the country's development, funding projects in the fields of agriculture, education and public health. U.S. support also has helped develop a labor framework and $100 million travel industry; funded efforts to preserve Cambodia's cultural heritage; and assisted in strengthening the electoral system, rule of law, political parties, the parliament and civil society. Many of these programs, including those carried out by the National Democratic Institute (NDI), have been supported by USAID, the National Endowment for Democracy and the Department of State's Bureau for Democracy, Human Rights and Labor.

NDI has focused its efforts in Cambodia on developing the country's system of governance and building a modern, more democratic political party system. Working in the country since 1992, NDI has worked at the local level to sponsor hundreds of community-level, multi-party dialogues, offering villagers the opportunity to voice their concerns to elected officials; sponsored election campaign debates throughout the country; assisted citizen organizations to build their capacity to monitor elections; and worked at the commune level to strengthen public participation in local governance. NDI has also assisted the efforts of ruling and opposition political parties to enhance their efforts to participate in elections; monitor polling sites on election day; develop greater opportunities for leadership by women and youth; and build more modern and democratic party structures. Other organizations have worked to promote women's economic and political empowerment, develop a more competent judicial system and train a cadre of professional journalists. In all of its work, NDI has engaged the major political parties and the ruling CPP has participated actively in all of the Institute's programs.

While serious development challenges remain, advances have been made, including improved health care, a better education system and the proliferation of an independent and active civil society. Although Cambodia is still a poor country, its economy has recently been growing at about seven7 percent. Cambodia's elections have never met international standards and have often been characterized by violence and intimidation; however, the 2017 commune council elections were a marked improvement over the past and experienced a turnout of slightly over 90 percent.

The Cambodian people have struggled, sometimes at great personal risk, to help advance the nation's economic and political development. However, the progress that has been made is unlikely to be sustained without the underpinning of a democratic process. The absence of a multi-party political system that helps ensure the accountability of public officials and provides a check on official corruption, as well as the lack of a free media and public participation in the political process, put the country's stability and further development at serious risk.

Cambodian officials have developed a "color revolution" narrative to justify their repressive measures. They claim that the opposition party was colluding with civil society, various individuals and foreign governments, including the U.S., to overthrow the regime. The narrative is based on the civil society-led movements in countries such as Serbia, Georgia, Kyrgyzstan, and Ukraine with claims that these were foreign-inspired attempts to replace legitimate governments with ones more acceptable to western democracies. In fact, these were movements that were organized to protect the integrity of elections, and their actions were triggered by massive electoral fraud engineered by authoritarian regimes. The so-called "people power" movements began in the Philippines in response to the effort by Ferdinand Marcos to steal the 1986 "snap" presidential election.

There is a more persuasive explanation for the government's repression. In hindsight, Cambodia's recent history provides strong evidence that the top leadership of the nation's ruling party has never been committed to a genuine democratic political process nor willing to accept defeat, or even the risk of defeat, at the polls. Since the transitional period began in 1991, the CPP has dominated the political landscape, maintaining control of the police, military, civil bureaucracy and virtually all of local government. However, the peace accords spawned a large number of civil society groups and they, as well as non-governmental organizations (NGOs) that have emerged since then, were able to operate most of the time with a surprising amount of freedom, given the dominance of the ruling party. Groups working on prison conditions, human rights, and even those monitoring the political process, as well as those engaged in areas like land rights and the environment, could criticize the government, especially in the English language press. Political parties, too, have had some space in which to operate, although the government used a variety of tactics, including the use of civil defamation suits, the party registration law and the filing of criminal charges, to keep them off balance.

According to a report by the Phnom Penh Post, Prime Minister Hun Sen has also allegedly resorted to purchasing social media followers, using so-called "click farms", in an attempt to show an increase in his popularity. The report showed that during a one month period last year, only 20 percent of the prime minister's new Facebook friends were from Cambodia -- most were from India, the Philippines and Brazil.

The political space open to critics of the government seemed to rely on the government's concern for its international standing, its reliance on foreign assistance and confidence that it could always resort to more coercive measures if its power was threatened. And, at key moments, those measures have been employed. In fact, since the Paris Peace Accords, Cambodia's political history might be considered as a period marked by three distinct "coups".

The first coup occurred when the results of the 1993 elections, conducted by the United Nations Transitional Authority in Cambodia (UNTAC), were overturned; UNTAC spent nearly $2 billion in organizing those polls. The CPP's leader, Hun Sen, alleged that the elections were rigged by the United Nations (UN). Rumors of a coup, and the threat of secession in several provinces along the border with Vietnam, led King Sihanouk to intervene. He proposed a power-sharing agreement that laid outside the nation's constitutional framework. Under the new arrangement, FUNCINPEC's leader, Prince Norodom Ranariddh, and the CPP's Hun Sen would hold the positions of First and Second Prime Minister, respectively. The government ministries also would be shared by each party. Post-UNTAC Cambodia began, then, with a government that did not reflect the outcome of the elections.

The second coup occurred in 1997, when Hun Sen brutally overthrew his coalition partner. Prince Ranariddh was charged with smuggling weapons into the country and conspiring with the outlawed Khmer Rouge. Dozens of FUNCINPEC supporters were killed during the coup; the offices of opposition political parties were sacked and burned; and an estimated 60,000 Cambodians fled to refugee camps in Thailand. The exiled opposition soon regrouped and formed the Union of Cambodian Democrats (UCD). Based in Thailand, the UCD in exile received support from the international community. NDI and the International Republican Institute (IRI) provided assistance designed to help the UCD remain unified and develop a negotiating strategy for their return to Cambodia.

The third coup, of course, occurred this year when the government disbanded the CNRP, the only opposition party that could effectively challenge them. The opposition's strength was clearly growing. In the 2013 national elections, the CNRP made a strong showing, increasing their seats in parliament from 29 to 55, while the CPP saw their representation decline from 90 to 68 seats. However, the newly elected opposition members refused to take their seats, alleging that over one million eligible voters had been omitted from the electoral rolls. Their claim was based, in part, on a civil society organization's audit of the voters' list, which had been conducted with NDI technical assistance. The ensuing crisis saw tens of thousands of CNRP supporters take to the streets. The 2013 elections demonstrated that the opposition CNRP was not only gaining in electoral strength, but that it also had the ability to mobilize large numbers of supporters.

In the elections' aftermath, the CPP-led government became increasingly repressive. In July of 2015, the National Assembly adopted the Law on Associations and Non-Governmental Organizations (LANGO). The law, which is widely viewed as designed to curtail civil society advocacy and political dissent, was passed despite the strong objections raised by Cambodian NGOs and the international community. Other actions by the government seemed designed to keep the opposition in disarray as local commune council elections, scheduled for 2017, approached. For example, shortly after LANGO was adopted, Kem Sokha was removed from the office of First Vice-President of the National Assembly; Kem Ley, a political activist and critic of the government was assassinated; the political party law was amended to permit the government to dissolve political parties when their leaders allegedly committed a crime; opposition leader Sam Rainsy was forced into exile; and Kem Sokha was convicted on politically-inspired charges. Sokha was later pardoned by King Sihamoni.

The CPP's motivation seems obvious. Its own internal polling, leaked to the press and reported in the local media, showed the ruling party facing tight races in upcoming local and national elections. Foreshadowing the CPP's electoral strategy, the party's poll, conducted by the Israel-based Shaviv Strategy and Campaigns, asked respondents "if Sam Rainsy is kept out of the country during the elections, would that make you more or less likely to vote for him?" and "if both Sam Rainsy and Kem Sokha left the country, who would you vote for?" and finally "if the CPP limits the CNRP from campaigning during the next elections, would that make it more or less likely to vote for the CNRP?" The poll also showed Hun Sen's favorability rating at 63 percent, compared to 84 percent for Sam Rainsy. Perhaps the most disturbing trend for the ruling CPP, according to the Phnom Penh Post, the poll found that a plurality of respondents would vote for the opposition in the upcoming commune council and national elections.

Commune council elections were held in June 2017, resulting in a strong showing for the opposition CNRP. The ruling CPP, which had long dominated the local governments, retained control of 1,156 of the 1,646 councils, but the CNRP increased their gains to 489 council chiefs from a previous 40. The CNRP had won 43.8 percent of the total votes cast, placing them in a strong position to contest in the 2018 national elections where they would be more competitive.

There was hope that the commune elections might usher in a period of greater political pluralism. For the first time, the opposition had a substantial presence in local government in the nation's heartland; the political parties had contested vigorously and relatively freely; the voter rolls had been improved and election authorities performed their responsibilities fairly and competently. That hope, however, was short lived.

In August 2017, the CPP's attention turned to international organizations which had been operating in Cambodia since the UNTAC era. Between August 16 and 23, Fresh News, a government online news outlet, reported on claims made on a Facebook page, Kon Khmer, that NDI was colluding with the opposition to overthrow the government and that the Institute was operating in the country illegally -- in violation of the NGO registration law. NDI received a notice from the government on August 23 ordering it to close its office and withdraw its international staff from the country within seven days. In the following days, the Voice of America (VOA) and Radio Free Asia (RFA) were also shuttered, as were dozens of local broadcast stations which carried VOA and RFA programming. The Cambodia Daily, the independent English language newspaper that had been operating since 1963, was forced to close when it received a $6.3 million tax bill from the government. These media outlets were the only source of traditional independent media that reached the interior of the country, where the opposition had recently performed well in the commune council elections.

Cambodian civil society and political leaders were also a target. Several civil society organizations were charged with bias under the vague provisions of LANGO and closed; staff of domestic monitoring groups and human rights organizations were intimidated and prevented from conducting their work; staff of NGOs working on sensitive issues such as the environment, land evictions and land grabbing have always been at risk and are especially vulnerable in the current political environment. On September 4, 2017, the political situation escalated when Kem Sokha was arrested in a midnight raid at his house and charged with treason. Since his arrest, almost one-half of the opposition's members of parliament have fled into exile. Since the dissolving of the CNRP, intimidation has continued. In early December, Prime Minister Hun Sen threatened to charge Sam Rainsy, exiled in Paris, with crimes after he urged the armed forces not to "shoot and kill innocent people" even if ordered to do so. Because of these repressive measures, an atmosphere of fear permeates the country.

The allegations against NDI were ironic because the Institute, which had been working in the country since 1992, engaged all the major parties, including the ruling CPP, in its programs. In fact, the morning that NDI received the letter ordering the closure of its office and expelling its international staff from the country, the Institute had met with a representative of the ruling party to plan its next training session with the CPP. Furthermore, the Ministry of Foreign Affairs had accepted NDI's registration documents a year earlier and has yet to act on the submission, whereas Article 14 of the Cambodia's Law on Non-Government Organizations requires the Ministry to make a decision on a registration application within 45 working days. NDI was in 3 frequent contact with the Ministry and other government offices concerning its registration status and at no time did the Cambodian government or any political party communicate to NDI any concerns about its programs or presence in the country. Moreover, NDI has a Memorandum of Understanding with the National Election Committee (NEC). It has worked closely with the NEC, as well as with the Interior Ministry in implementing the Institute's village-based political participation programs.

The Cambodian government's repressive actions are clearly designed to maintain the ruling party in power; Prime Minister Hun Sen has repeatedly said that he wants to continue in office beyond his 32-year reign. He has also warned of civil war if the ruling CPP was voted out of office. However, the government's actions may also represent a strategic realignment, placing Cambodia more firmly in China's orbit. While the Cambodian government was widely condemned by the international community for its recent repressive measures, China was quick to offer support, ignoring the provisions of the Paris Peace Agreement to which it is a signatory. Following the dissolution of the CNRP, China's Foreign Minister, Wang Yi stated that "China supports the Cambodian side's efforts to protect political stability and achieve economic development, and believes that the Cambodian government can lead people to deal with domestic and foreign challenges and smoothly hold elections next year." The Chinese and Cambodian governments have also reportedly agreed to cooperate in a joint think tank to study so-called the color revolutions.

During the past decade, China has been steadily increasing its influence in Cambodia through foreign investments in infrastructure projects such as dams and highways, as well as in mines and textiles. Chinese firms are involved in building apartment buildings, luxury condos and hospitals. While the U.S. remains Cambodia's largest export market, China has become the country's largest provider of bilateral aid. A spokesman for Cambodia's Council of Ministers was recently quoted as saying, "without Chinese aid, we go nowhere." In addition, Cambodia's security cooperation with China is expanding, while it is contracting with the U.S. In 2016, China and Cambodia conducted their first bilateral military exercise. The following year, Cambodia cancelled Ankor Sentinel, an annual military exercise with the U.S., and also terminated a long-standing Navy Seabees humanitarian program. China provided 60 percent of Cambodia's arms purchases in 2013 and also provides equipment and training to Cambodia's military. In return, Cambodia has acted as an ally within the Association of Southeast Asian Nations (ASEAN), effectively preventing the body from achieving consensus on issues related to territorial claims in the South China Sea.

Whether a strategic realignment would be popular with the Cambodian people is unclear. One poll conducted in March, 2017 found that 80.7 percent of Cambodians had either a favorable or very favorable view of the U.S., compared to 66.2 percent for China.

Mr. Chairman, it is not too late for the Cambodian government to reverse its course. Fresh elections should be held and the Cambodian people allowed to choose their leaders in a credible electoral process. No Cambodian government elected under the current circumstances would have any claim to legitimacy.

In order to establish the conditions in which credible elections could be held, measures the Cambodian government must implement include: reinstating the CNRP as a legal entity; immediately releasing Kem Sokha and permitting Sam Rainsy and other CNRP leaders to return from exile; freeing all political prisoners, including civil society leaders and political activists; allowing journalists and media outlets to operate free of violence and intimidation, including VOA, RFA and The Cambodia Daily; permitting domestic and international election observer groups free access to monitor all aspects of the electoral process; and forming a new election commission that includes members of the opposition.

Much work would need to be done to build a level of trust between the ruling and opposition parties, beginning with the government making a firm commitment to cease all forms of violence and intimidation and permitting domestic and international organizations to monitor political conditions in the county in order to help ensure that the pledge is kept. In addition, there must be sufficient time before elections are held to permit the opposition to reassemble in Cambodia, organize and compete.

There has been widespread condemnation of the Cambodian government's recent actions from governments and organizations throughout the world, ranging from the European Union (EU), Sweden and Australia to the Inter-Parliamentary Union, the French Senate, Human Rights Watch, and the editorial pages of the Washington Post, New York Times and newspapers around the globe. Their statements help to bolster the resolve of those affected by this crisis and hopefully will continue as long as the current situation persists.

I want to recognize the U.S. Congress, the White House, State Department, and the U.S. Embassy and U.S. Agency for International Development (USAID) mission in Phnom Penh for their strong and timely statements in support of democracy in Cambodia, and for the appropriate actions taken by the U.S. government in terminating assistance to Cambodia's election commission and imposing visa restrictions on those Cambodian officials responsible for undermining democracy. These words and actions are important because they demonstrate that concrete measures will be taken unless certain conditions for the return to a democratic process are met.

There are other actions that the international community should consider until political conditions in Cambodia show marked improvement. These include:

> **1. Consider the withdrawal or suspension of all but humanitarian aid to the Cambodian government until the conditions for the return to democracy are met.** At a minimum those conditions should be the release from custody of Kem Sokha and allowing Sam Rainsy to return from exile, as well as dropping the politically motivated charges against the CNRP leaders. Further conditions should include insisting that the Cambodian government cease all intimidation of its political opponents and permit all exiled opposition party leaders to return to their seats in the National Assembly and local councils. The government also must permit the news media to operate freely, including VOA, RFA and The Cambodia Daily. Civil society workers must be freed from custody and allowed to perform their work without intimidation.

2. Continue to support the work of non-governmental organizations (NGOs) within Cambodia. NGOs working within the country are especially vulnerable to government reprisals and need the continued support of the international community to carry on their work. These include not only organizations that focus on the political process but also groups that work on sensitive issues such as deforestation, land grabbing and human trafficking. Government repression coupled with a loss of international funding would be especially tragic for organizations that conduct critical work.

3. Review the possibility of altering the terms of trade with Cambodia. As previously stated, the U.S. is the largest export market for Cambodian goods, receiving 25 percent of Cambodia's exports; the EU is the next largest. This is the area in which the international community perhaps has the most leverage for inducing positive change.

4. Continue international engagement -- such as the international response to Cambodia's 1997 coup. Following that coup, an informal diplomatic network, known as the Friends of Cambodia Group, helped Hun Sen and the political opposition come to an agreement on the conditions under which the exiles would return to Cambodia to participate in national elections the following year. The UN accreditation committee decided that Cambodia's seat in the General Assembly should remain vacant, thereby withholding UN recognition of the government at that time. Similar moves might help pave the way for new negotiations.

5. Support exiled political leaders' efforts to negotiate their return. Despite their current condition, the CNRP opposition remains a legitimate and important political force within Cambodia, having recently received over three million votes in the commune council elections. However, over 100 opposition activists and elected officials are in exile, largely scattered throughout three countries: the U.S., Australia and Thailand. They currently lack the ability to remain a cohesive force. As in 1997, continued support should be provided to the CNRP leadership to help them convene, and communicate with their supporters and the international community.

6. Assist efforts to engage international financial institutions, as well as global and regional bodies on the Cambodia issue. The U.S. and other like-minded governments should use their influence, and support the efforts of others, in engaging all of these bodies to help ensure that they understand the political situation in Cambodia from the broadest viewpoints, including Cambodia's political opposition, and are not only hearing the Cambodian government's narrative. The international community also should consider what actions these institutions might take in helping to resolve the crisis.

Institutions, such as the UN, can speak with a moral force and have the experience and ability to provide a forum where contending political forces can at least begin to discuss the future. The UN should also engage because it is the legacy of UNTAC that is threatened. Regional bodies such as ASEAN can play a role in mediation, and there is precedent for its engagement. ASEAN issued a strong statement following the 1997 coup, and postponed Cambodia's membership application which was pending when that coup occurred. Financial institutions, such as the World Bank and International Monetary Fund also have precedents for taking actions when political instability could lead to an unfavorable investment climate.

Mr. Chairman, I want to thank the Committee for your interest and concern. The international community and the Cambodian people have invested a great deal in efforts to build a stable, democratic and prosperous Cambodia since 1991. Very few countries suffered more violence in the 20th century than Cambodia, and its people deserve the democratic future envisioned in the 1991 accords.

Mr. YOHO. Thank you for your testimony, all of you. I appreciate it.

Everybody has brought up the elections of 2013 and the elections last summer, this past summer, that resoundingly showed the will of the people, you know, is what we saw with the numbers that are favored and the growing popularity and the growth of the CNRP. I think this speaks loudly. But what we are seeing is, we are seeing the world divide diametrically opposed philosophies with Western ideologies.

The universal principles—and, Ms. Kem, you brought up what we believe here in America, but I think if we all look at people around the world, and I have had the opportunity to speak to people all over, there is innate beliefs that we all have: Liberty, freedom, self-will, self-determination. Those are universal beliefs that, I believe—my beliefs are that everybody has those in the world.

Where we start dividing this or start bringing—preventing this is when you have authoritarian governments. And, you know, we look at the beliefs that we have here that government is by the people, to serve the people, versus the authoritarian type that we are seeing, especially with the rise of China after the 19th Congress, where Xi Jinping said the era of China has come and it is time to take the center stage of the world. And I just I read an article where they said the purpose of the citizens, their sole purpose is to serve the government.

You know, in our forum, we have the government is there to serve the many. Whereas, theirs—their people are to serve the government of a few. And we know those regimes don't last longterm.

And, you know, saying that, I look at the amount of aid we have given Cambodia. My figures show from 1993 to 2016, aid to Cambodia was $1.7 billion in aggregate aid. One-point-seven billion dollars. A lot of this goes in the name of good governance, building democracies. And it is something that we can't wish upon another country, but we know it works pretty darn well here. It has for the last 226 in our constitutional republic. And it is something that we know, again, that the innate feeling of people everywhere want what we have, and so we have invested in this.

What I would like to know from you is, what programs have you seen work the best? And we will start with you, Ms. Kem. Your feelings with the investment that we have made—the American people have made. What is your opinion on where we should keep going or should we just pull back and pull back everything?

Ms. KEM. Thank you, Chairman, for the question. I think what is most helpful so far in Cambodia is a democracy program that involves direct citizen participation. I can give one example of the Cambodian Center for Human Rights, which was funded, and I believe still funded, partly by USAID in some form. So any program that works directly and encouraging people, empowering people to understand their rights, to stand up for their freedom.

And, also, I would say, number two, because of the timing of the election, any program that works with NGOs, that works on election-related matters, whether it is investigation or monitoring of election.

Mr. YOHO. Is that possible now that he has cracked down on everything, you know, and gotten rid of the opposition party? Is that possible to do that in that country?

Ms. KEM. There are still a few effective organizations. For example, COMFREL, they work on elections, and I believe that their job is extremely important, as important as the presence of the opposition. They are an election watchdog and their work has been significant. For example, in 2013, without their documentation, we would not have known all the——

Mr. YOHO. And their job may be easier in the next election, right, because there is no other party other than the one he is going to allow run.

Ms. KEM. In the case that there will be election, we want to be prepared that these watchdogs are equipped with the right knowledge and right tools to do their job.

Mr. YOHO. All right. Given the actions of Hun Sen and the regime has taken against the CNRP, what is the opposition's current plan of action?

Ms. KEM. We have two things, really. We have the Cambodian people inside a country, but as of right now, there is very little they can do because of physical threats, really. So another channel for us would be through the international community. And I believe in the Cambodian context, the donor community has more of an obligation than any other country because of the Paris Peace Accord binding.

So for us, we will continue to advocate for the reinstatement of our party. And, again, timing is of essence. If there is no solution soon—soon, we are talking about the end of this year, or the latest I would say at the end of next month—then any possibility of free and fair election is impossible. Then we would have to rethink, so what is next. And I think the international community and the Cambodian people together will pave a way for us to go back and restore democracy.

Mr. YOHO. Okay. Thank you.

I am going to turn to the ranking member and let him ask his questions. Thank you.

Mr. SHERMAN. Ms. Kem, how would you describe the current status of your father, Kem Sokha, the head of the CNRP? We know he was arrested on this ridiculous charge of treason. And how can the United States and the international community work to ensure that he is treated justly and released?

Ms. KEM. So far, I believe that they deny any visit access from outside. The only people that can visit him is my mother and his lawyers. He is kept in solitary confinement, and he has no access to the outside world, except through my mother. And I believe what the U.S. can do is continue—the U.S. and its allies, meaning the EU, Japan, and the other countries, is continue to press for at least a visit to see how he is doing. And also to communicate already to the Cambodian Government about any repercussions should they mistreat him. I think that is very important to preempt.

Mr. SHERMAN. Has he been denied medical attention or pharmaceuticals?

Ms. KEM. So far, I believe a group of doctors has seen him once.

Mr. SHERMAN. Mr. Wollack outlined a number of steps that we would consider. I think it is now time for us to step up to the business community in the United States and hopefully get European governments to do the same, and Japan's governments to do the same, to put in American law that says, if we decide to forego this special access to U.S. markets, that any company buying garments from Cambodia can immediately void its contract. So we can put that in as a matter of law, that is deemed by law to apply to any contract, and we can demand that no U.S. company can sign a contract in the future that doesn't specify that, so that there is no doubt that it applies. That would have the effect of putting every garment manufacturer in Cambodia on notice that their contracts are hanging by a thread.

Ms. Enos, how dependent is Cambodia upon its ability to export garments to Europe, Japan, and the United States?

Ms. ENOS. Well, I would say that one of my concerns with pursuing this type of strategy would be that it has the potential to harm the Cambodian people more than to——

Mr. SHERMAN. Keep in mind, it dramatically helps the people of Africa, dramatically helps the people of South Asia. We are only going to buy a certain number of shirts. I know your focus is on helping the people of Cambodia, but what we give to Cambodian manufacturers undermines democracy in Cambodia and takes jobs away from sub-Saharan Africa.

Again, Mr. Wollack, do you have an answer on just how dependent the Cambodian Government is?

Mr. WOLLACK. They are very, very dependent. My only recommendation would be on these issues of sanctions. As we——

Mr. SHERMAN. And notice, I wasn't saying sanctions. I was saying let us have contractual provisions so that if in the future we have sanctions, we don't have American companies in violation of contracts. Go ahead.

Mr. WOLLACK. My only recommendation would be, as we did in South Africa, as we do in Venezuela, in Cuba and other places, is to consult with local democrats, those in Phnom Penh and those outside the country.

Mr. SHERMAN. Including one sitting next to you, yes.

Mr. WOLLACK. Exactly. To hear their views and——

Mr. SHERMAN. I mean, the next step is to be legally prepared to move forward. That sends a message and hopefully will result in the changes, because we propose steps we can take against individuals. Well, I am not sure they want to go to Disneyland, and even if they do they can go to Shanghai.

We talked about cutting off foreign aid. I am not sure that that will get the attention. Their focus is on maintaining power. So we have to at least prepare the ground for something that goes beyond that. Now, NDI has been kicked out. Is RII still operating in Cambodia?

Mr. WOLLACK. Well, RII did not have international staff in Cambodia to——

Mr. SHERMAN. Are they moving in to fill in for you?

Mr. WOLLACK. Well, I doubt whether that will be the case because they have been under—they are under attack.

Mr. SHERMAN. So it is not like they are just going to go after the D. They are willing to go after the organization affiliated with the President's party as well.

Mr. WOLLACK. Yes. They have been attacked rather vociferously over the last few months as well.

Mr. SHERMAN. I yield back.

Mr. YOHO. Thank you. We will next go to Mr. Rohrabacher from California.

Mr. ROHRABACHER. I think that, well, number one, we are sending a message by this, as I mentioned in my first 5 minutes, and it is important that that message is very clear. Hun Sen has got to go. The United States is on the side of the Cambodian people who want a more democratic and honest government, and that is that. That is the number one message.

So, number two, about this hearing, maybe we can get down to some brass tacks on something that we can do. And let me just say, after my long period of time that I have been friends of the Cambodian community here and the Cambodian people, one message I would like to send to them is America just can't do it for you. This is not going to be a gift.

Every time I talk to my Cambodian friends, they are saying, well, when are the Marines going to come and get rid of Hun Sen so we can then take over the government and have free elections? It ain't going to happen. So we have got to find—that is number two message: Don't wait for the American military might to displace Hun Sen.

So what is the third step? So what do we do with Hun Sen? What do we do? What is the exact pattern? Ms. Kem, you gave some very good suggestions there. I am going to get into a little detail on it now. Maybe we should have, Mr. Chairman, a list of individuals in the Cambodian Government and corporations, both individuals and corporations that are from other countries, who are there profiting from the corruption of the Hun Sen regime. And there should be some kind of economic sanctions on them. It is like the Magnitsky Act, so to speak.

Now, right now there is a lot of—for example, there are big problems I know of in Cambodia where people's property is being stolen, and it is being handed over to cronies of Mr. Hun Sen, both national and international cronies, I might add.

So, thus, we need a list from you. We need the Cambodian community to provide us a list of specific corporations and individuals, and then we can work on legislation that will require our State Department to investigate these particular individuals, and basically will be able to tell us, does this person deserve specific sanctions? Like when I say this is sort of the Magnitsky Act, but I think it goes beyond that, because this is just simply a situation where we also are talking about economic crimes as well as political crimes and as well as just regular criminal activity by people murdering their opposition.

So if you can give us, let's say out of this hearing that we get a commitment to get some names of people that we then can ask for and legally require our State Department to do an analysis of what the particular person has done and to verify that it will be

justified for sanctions against the individual. So that is one thing
I would hope would come out of this today.

And, again, let me just say that it is not just the United States
that isn't going to do it for you. It is not Japan that is going to do
it for you. We also need to see some signs of some resistance among
the Cambodian people to their government. It is not their government. If it was their government, we wouldn't want resistance to
it. It is a clique that is holding power by force and corruption, and
they are not your government. They are gangsters, and we need to
recognize that. And gangsters understand two things: Brute force
and a deal.

Now I am going to ask you one last thing about the deal. I want
your opinion on this. Maybe the only way—I remember about 20
years ago, I sat across from Hun Sen at a table. And I told him,
I said, you know, we are all getting a little older here and we want
to have time to enjoy our lives. I will make you a deal. I will retire
from Congress if you will retire from being the President of Cambodia. He didn't take——

Mr. YOHO. You are still here.

Mr. ROHRABACHER. He didn't take me up and I am here too, so
there we go. But maybe we could, again, maybe some people should
approach Hun Sen and just give him the deal. And I would like
your opinion on this.

Should we offer Hun Sen a deal, this happens with all tyrants,
by the way, that says, get out of town and you can keep your ill-
gotten gains. We are not going to bother you, but get out of there,
and as compared to if we don't, we say, no, the only way you are
going to get out of there is if we kill you or if we capture you and
put you in a cage. That guy is never going to go voluntarily.

So what do you think about offering Hun Sen a deal, get out of
there, let the people have democracy, and you will be free from
being prosecuted?

I would just like a short answer from each of you, please.

Ms. ENOS. Sure. I think the critical role of the U.S. Government
is to restore freedom to the Cambodian people. And so I think
strengthening democratic institutions is probably the best way to
do that. And I think that holding accountable individuals, including
Hun Sen and other individuals within the Cambodian Government,
is the best way to do that.

I don't know that we need to offer him a specific deal. I think
we just need to put pressure on key nodes and facets of democracy
in Cambodia.

Mr. ROHRABACHER. Okay. So you would oppose the idea of just
offering him a deal?

Ms. ENOS. Yes.

Mr. ROHRABACHER. Get out of town—get out of town and let us
get on with our freedom.

What about you, Ms. Kem?

Ms. KEM. First of all, I agree with the list of individuals and corporations that are undermining democracy in Cambodia, and we
will happily provide you with that list.

In terms of a deal, I think right now he is not ready for a deal.
You need to corner him first, and then he will propose a deal himself.

Mr. ROHRABACHER. Okay. Well, what if he proposes the deal? Let me get out of town with my money.

Ms. KEM. His current state of mind is not about receiving a deal yet. It is about crushing the rest of the opposition that is left.

Mr. ROHRABACHER. Sure. The secret is is we want to get him to the point where he is either going to ask for a deal or we can get rid of him ourselves. But—so you are sort of hedging a little bit here.

Ms. KEM. No, I don't think I am hedging.

Mr. ROHRABACHER. You said yet, we don't want to offer him a deal yet.

Ms. KEM. When he is ready to make a deal, he will offer the deal. Right now I think what it is important, to put pressure on him. I agree with Olivia. And I think maybe I am more optimistic than some of you. I believe that individual targeted sanctions alone will likely be enough. You may not have to pull the nuclear option of removing Cambodia's trade privileges. I really strongly believe that.

So let's just start with the individual financial sanctions. That will put tremendous pressure. And I must say even the visa ban alone, it impacts him a lot. It is not just about Disneyland.

Mr. ROHRABACHER. Okay. All right.

Ms. KEM. It is much more than that. It makes their life difficult. And if you move on to financial sanctions, I think that alone will have enough impact for them to reconsider.

Mr. ROHRABACHER. Usually people like Hun—well, gangsters, I will just say usually gangster regimes understand a deal when there is a gun at their head, but that is another issue.

What about it? Should we offer him a deal or not?

Mr. WOLLACK. I would say, it may not only be the Prime Minister. There is more than just an individual. And I am a big believer in institutions and processes, and I like to believe that these types of deals would be entered into by democratically elected governments, that they have the right and the authority and the legitimacy——

Mr. ROHRABACHER. Oh, sure.

Mr. WOLLACK [continuing]. To deal with those that their nondemocratic predecessors.

Mr. ROHRABACHER. Well, whatever deal would have to—whatever deal would be offered, if there is a deal—I am not, by the way, advocating that necessarily. I just was interested in your opinion. But it has to be something that could be then accepted by the democratically elected government.

Mr. WOLLACK. And I think broader negotiations are necessary, because I think it is beyond just one individual. I think you have the military. You have the deep state. You have other aspects of the political system that would have to be part of a negotiated settlement.

Mr. ROHRABACHER. Thank you.

Mr. YOHO. Maybe we can get him a signed copy of the art of the deal.

Mr. Lowenthal.

Mr. LOWENTHAL. Thank you, Mr. Chair. And I would just like to say I have a deal for you too.

I think I really like the direction that we are going in. We are trying to figure out what can we do now, and I think that is critically important. And we are seeing that there is no easy silver bullet to do it.

We have talked about increasing what the State Department sanctions are by looking at increasing sanctions on individuals, on businesses that engage in these behaviors. I think that is very appropriate to look at.

I would like to raise some other things that I have heard so far this morning to really talk about where we can go. One is, how do we do it to reconstitute the Paris Agreement? There were all the signatures. There were 15. We were one of the signatures. All of the people that we are talking about also signed the Paris Agreement that they would ensure free and fair elections.

What do we do now—what do we do now to make sure—and is there a path to do it? I would like to hear from you.

That is my first question. Is that an option, and how do we do that? Anybody want to choose to answer it? Ms. Enos.

Ms. ENOS. I think that already there are Ambassadors from several of the signatories of the Paris Peace Agreement that do meet together to sort of convene. I think we should sort of raise the profile of this and perhaps have foreign ministry-level officials come together and talk about what are the long-term as well as the short-term steps to ensuring that Cambodia gets back on track.

Mr. LOWENTHAL. Do you see us as a Congress writing to our State Department and asking them to reconvene or to raise this issue with the foreign ministers possibly, our U.N. Ambassador also raising? Because I am trying to figure out how do we get there? And so that is very good.

So we need some mechanism to reach these foreign ministers of the countries that have already signed their signatures to see what they think how we can work together and to entreat. So that is one.

Mr. WOLLACK. An alternative too is the Friends of Cambodia group that was brought together following the 1997 coup.

Mr. LOWENTHAL. Okay.

Mr. WOLLACK. That group supported the negotiations that ultimately led for the then-UCD opposition to return to Cambodia. And I think even before that, however, what is necessary, the opposition right now, the leadership of the opposition, aside from being in jail, are scattered in Australia, Thailand, the United States. International support has to be extended to them so they can communicate to the international community. This is a coalition. This is not a single party. And they have to communicate with their supporters in the country. They have to communicate with the international community.

Right now, the government is the only body that is communicating in multilateral settings. And they have to begin discussing and convening to discuss how they would return to Cambodia, under what conditions. And the international community, Friends of Cambodia, can help that happen as well.

Ms. KEM. I am largely exploring myself the path to revive the spirit of the Paris Peace Accord, and I believe it may fall under the jurisdiction of the U.N. Security Council. So I am trying to meet with the missions at the U.N. who have membership, permanent membership in the National Security Council. And I think they have the authority or more, I would say more obligation about reviving the Paris Peace Accords. So I think that is one way to look at it.

And I agree with Olivia about at least you can convene minister, foreign minister-level of the key signatories. It doesn't have to be all the countries. And right now, even on ambassadorial level, it is not that coordinated yet. So I think that is the message that each government or the U.S. Government, I believe maybe the French Government as well can begin, can start to look into.

Mr. LOWENTHAL. Following that, talking about this international consortium, whether it was through the Paris—and I think it was you, Mr. Wollack, talked about trade. Now, we are talking about individual sanctions from the United States, but I think also you mentioned that the vast majority of Cambodians' exports go to either the United States, the EU, or to Japan. How can we use that as leverage, that kind of trade that goes, in terms of trade agreements or other things? Maybe you can explain or anyone else. The leverage that we have is that we are buying all their goods. It is not just from the bad folks. We are buying all the Cambodian goods, EU, United States and Japan. How do we use that? Do you have some ideas?

Mr. WOLLACK. Well, I am not a trade expert, but what I would recommend, there are a lot of options of how to tie trade in. The international financial institutions, by the way, put a number of loans on hold to Cambodia because of land expulsions. They then extended it a little later and they came under criticism.

So the international financial institutions have a role to play here too when it comes to investment opportunities in the country. But I think on the trade issues, there are a variety of options, but I think this is an issue that requires consultation with the Cambodians first before we get into how to do it, to determine what they feel comfortable with so it doesn't harm the Cambodian people.

And different democratic forces in different countries take different positions on this issue, but I think they should be sort of the driving force in the types of recommendations that they would make to the international community on the issues of trade.

Ms. KEM. I think you can first start by the reviewing process. Reviewing, identifying the violation, and then do a recommendation and communicate that very clearly and strongly to the Cambodian Government. And, again, I am optimistic and I think that alone will be enough.

And I wouldn't call that a bluff or a threat either. It is just preparing ground. If you really need to pull it, if the actions by the Cambodian Government really violate those terms and conditions of the trade, then you may have to pull—to cancel the trade.

But I think reviewing, it is very important to start the reviewing process. And I urge the same thing with the EU as well. Both the EU and the U.S. can start reviewing the trade privileges and the violation that the Cambodian Government is conducting.

Ms. ENOS. I think it is critical that we be as targeted as possible in what we are reviewing and what we are thinking of doing, in terms of action toward Cambodia. One of the concerns that I have with doing a broader trade review, which I agree with Mona would be good to review it.

But to actually revoke all those trade preferences is that it is not clear that it is a direct response to threats to democracy and human rights. When you target specific individuals, when you review democracy assistance, you are considering things that are directly relevant to the challenges at hand. And I think that sends a much clearer message that U.S. policy will respond in kind to the ways that there are violations that are occurring.

Mr. LOWENTHAL. Thank you, Mr. Chair. Do I have any time left or——

Mr. YOHO. Yes, go ahead.

Mr. LOWENTHAL. Thank you.

The one other question is, you know, I have also talked about, you know, we do provide a significant—I think the chairman mentioned the amount of aid that we have given in terms of foreign aid over.

But it seems to me, in my understanding—I would like to hear from the panel—that U.S. foreign aid primarily has gone to NGOs and to organizations trying to bring about change in Cambodia rather than directly to the government. And that if we look at restricting foreign aid, it may not impact the government as much as those people that are already seeking democracy.

So I would like to know do you see that as, you know, something that we should be very much aware of if we move in that direction also? And I would like to hear your comments on that.

Ms. ENOS. I think it is critical that if we are going to do a review of our democracy programming that we make sure that we keep in place programs that encourage development of civil society and encourage the development of democratic institutions.

I think it is true that a lot of the aid does go toward NGOs. And this brings me to one point that I think is critical. Even though the U.S. has withdrawn support for the 2018 elections, I think it is still critical that some of these election-monitoring NGOs be allowed, possibly even encouraged, to operate, just without U.S. assistance, because I think we need to be able to get a pulse on to what extent democratic institutions in Cambodia have regressed, and also to sort of get a pulse on what is the public opinion in Cambodia toward Hun Sen, toward the CPP. And I think if you don't have election-monitoring organizations from the U.S. or from other Western governments there, you will lose that critical insight.

But even still, I think that is still reason to review our democracy programming in Cambodia and make sure that it is achieving the outcomes that we want and that it is bolstering the right institutions, not being diverted, because aid is always fungible. So watch that.

Mr. LOWENTHAL. Thank you.

Ms. KEM. I would say that do not underestimate your leverages. If you look at, was it last month when the U.S. announced it was pulling support for demining for the National Commission, CMAC— I can't think of the full name now—and giving that money instead to NGO who also work on demining, that alone got the Cambodian Government panicking. And that is only I believe $2 million a year. You would think that is a very small number of money in the U.S. context. But I believe that the aid that goes directly—I am talking about the one that goes directly to Central Cambodian Government, if you cut that, it will have an impact.

Sure, they will supplement that either from China or from other sources, but that would still hurt them and hurt the Cambodian Government itself, and would have to reconsider—I think they will have to reconsider their action.

And I agree with Olivia also that the U.S. should still continue to monitor the electoral environment in the case that the election go forward and regardless what kind of election we would have in 2018. So I think an election monitoring program is still very important, because you want to document what is going on, to have an opinion on it, regardless of the circumstances.

Mr. WOLLACK. I would just add that monitoring the election process by citizen monitoring groups does not necessarily legitimize the process; rather, it legitimizes themselves. And so the worst thing is to withdraw assistance so they are under extraordinary pressure by the government. It would be even worse if the international community suddenly withdrew support for these groups.

There are many other areas in assistance that we have provided Cambodia over the years. We funded projects in the field, as Mona said, in demining, but also agriculture, education, and public health. We have helped develop a labor framework and a $100 million travel industry. We supported Cambodia's cultural heritage. So there is a myriad of programs, I think important programs over the years that have had some important impact, and those I think can certainly be reviewed.

Mr. LOWENTHAL. Thank you. And just as I yield back, I would just like to say, in addition to the statements that you have done at the beginning, you have provided us with a number of specific recommendations. It would be very helpful if you could provide those to the committee or to members of the committee, because really, that is where the next step is.

And we are trying to figure out what is the next step, and you have a wealth of information that you have provided us. And I would like it as concretely as possible to provide to the committee. Thank you.

Mr. YOHO. Thank you. I appreciate your extra input. We allowed people to go over extra because we are down to a few people, but it is more engaging this way and we are getting more information out.

We are going to go back to Mr. Rohrabacher. He has some comments.

Mr. ROHRABACHER. Just a couple thoughts. And if we have a list of names of people that should be investigated and to see if they are engaged in human rights abuses, but also in total corruption and harmful corruption to their society, those names should be provided to the chairman of this subcommittee. He has a staff, and we have just talked about it and the staff will look at that and make sure that we follow through with legislation, talking to the State Department. Then you have the staff here would be able to follow through and make sure we get something done there.

Second of all, about general sanctions versus specific sanctions. I am sorry that when you have a dictatorship, do you think that Hun Sen would give a damn about whether or not some people were being hurt down in his country by a sanction? Do you think he does? No. Why should he? In fact, his gang is buffeted. They are not going to get—they are not going to not have an extra bowl of rice because of sanctions. They have already got their money and they have got—and whatever income is going on. They are the ones who are ripping off the profit of the whole country rather than having it become part of the ownership of the people.

And number two, of course, if there were any sanctions that did— general sanctions, another monstrous gangster regime called Beijing will step in and take care of, oh, well, we will come in and do this. And I am sorry, all the really good industries that you were talking about that were—you know, I am sure that it is Hun Sen's buddies that have got the permits to operate those particular businesses. That is the way it works.

And, again, you have got to hold people accountable. I do think the people of Cambodia will reach a breaking point where they will have to at some point say, we are going to be engaged in something that will force Hun Sen out and we can't just rely on other people, whether they are Japanese-Americans or ASEAN friends or whatever.

The people of Cambodia either are going to stand up to Hun Sen and kick his butt out of there or he is going to continue in power. We can, put even, what I am suggesting by holding specific people accountable for their crimes, I don't think that will result in Hun Sen running off unless, of course, a deal is made, which, of course, we thought about that too.

Well, thank you very much, Mr. Chairman.

Thank you to the witnesses as well.

Mr. YOHO. Well thank you for both of your input. Thank you. Let me ask real briefly, how effective is Radio Free Asia, Voice of America, or other transmissions into Cambodia, in your opinion, Ms. Enos?

Ms. ENOS. Radio Free Asia and Voice of America are critical to ensuring that democracy continues to flourish in Cambodia. They provide an alternative news source, and they help to encourage the sort of domestic news sources that are already there.

So I think it is really a shame that Radio Free Asia has had to withdraw its service, and my understanding is that VOA has also had to reduce what it can provide as well.

Mr. YOHO. I would assume that most people in Cambodia know that CNRP has been kicked out, right? In all of the regions, everybody is aware of that?

I would think they would be highly inflamed about that and irritated. That is a program that we think is very effective. Anybody have a differing opinion?

Mr. WOLLACK. Particularly in the heartland of the country too, these outlets are extremely important.

Mr. YOHO. Okay. And like I said in the beginning, what we see over and over again is the same thing playing, you know, the good versus evil. And I think it was 2½ years ago I was at—I think you were there. It was a meeting with a lot of our active and retired generals. And they said that the world was going through a tectonic shift in superpowers or world powers that we haven't seen prior to World War II.

And I think we are seeing this played out. I think China is in another phase. I don't want to say it is phase two or phase three of their grand scheme. And I see them putting pressure on countries around the world, in this instance in Cambodia. Wherever there is a democracy, they see that as a threat and they have a hand in that. And if you see a democracy stumbling, falling, you can look at—China is in the background.

How much influence, in your opinion, has China invoked on the current breakdown of the free elections of democracy and the disbanding of the CNRP? If you guys don't mind, we will just go through.

Mr. Wollack, you can start. You look like you are ready.

Mr. WOLLACK. Well, no. I just say that China has given a good deal of support. It has also—the Cambodian Government has reciprocated, particularly in ASEAN forums, where they blocked any effort to reach consensus on the South China Sea.

It was interesting that China and Cambodia announced that they were going to set up a joint think tank to study color revolutions, because this is the narrative that somehow the West was trying to instigate a color revolution and domestic groups were as well.

And I think if this think tank did accurate research, they would find out one very fundamental point, that the movements that rose up in places like the Philippines in 1986, in Kyrgyzstan, and Serbia, and Ukraine, and Georgia were the result of one thing, and that was a stolen election. Movements rose up, starting with the People Power Revolution in the Philippines, because authoritarian regimes stole an election. It had nothing to do with outside intervention.

And so I think it serves Cambodian interests and stability in the country, and in terms of China its view of stability in the region, to have an election that is seen by the people of Cambodia to reflect their will.

Mr. YOHO. Ms. Kem.

Ms. KEM. I don't think that China can replace the role of, for example, the EU or the U.S. has on Cambodia's economy. China is not the one that is buying our products. And over 70 percent of Cambodian exports depend on U.S. and EU market. And I am sure you have seen in other closed society around the world in the region, they can't survive on China's support alone.

And then number two, do you, meaning the free world, the U.S. or the EU, do you sit back and allow China to go forward with the aggression or you fight for your space, because it is in your interest as well, as I made my remark earlier, to stay connected in the region.

I think Cambodia could be an easy case and a good opportunity for the U.S. to take leadership in the region and to show that democracy can win. And it is very, very possible. I believe elsewhere in the region, it may be more difficult. In Cambodia, you just have to lift your finger. And, again, I am more optimistic than some of you. I believe that there is a lot of hope, and I think that it can be done very soon as well.

Mr. YOHO. Ms. Enos.

Ms. ENOS. I think China has consistently proven a bad actor in Cambodia, and that is evidenced by the latest statement by Chinese Foreign Minister Wang Yi, which affirmed Cambodia's decision to dissolve the opposition party.

Not only that, but, as Mr. Wollack referenced, in ASEAN, they had sort of a tit-for-tat agreement where Cambodia was, I mean it looks like basically paid off in order to disavow the South China Sea resolution that ASEAN had made. And I think it is to the tune of $237 million in direct aid, $90 million in forgiven debt, and $15 million in other forms of assistance that they decided to give to Cambodia.

So I think China has proven to be a consistently bad actor and sort of acts with sort of impunity and with total disregard to what is going on in Cambodia. But I would echo Mona's sentiments that I think, apart from U.S. leadership—and this includes with forming the Paris Peace Agreement—you are not going to see substantive action being taken, because I think the U.S. needs to call upon EU partners, needs to call upon Japan and other signatories that have demonstrated an interest in seeing Cambodia get back on the track toward reform.

Mr. YOHO. No, I think you are absolutely right. And, you know, China is pushing that, because they want control of that region. And we see them with the power of, you know, of the ASEAN nations. Just one nation can shut down the rest of them. And this is something we are looking at, you know, talking to the ASEAN nations and seeing if we need to kind of see what we can do to put pressure on an individual nation that is doing this, because that was about $368 million that you said that gave them.

Again, this comes down to—and I wanted to talk to you about—you were talking about the United States has to keep pushing and giving them and helping with democracies and that. I kind of take a different angle on that. I can't give you democracy. I can help you get it, but you have to have the want and the desire.

It is like my mom wanted me to play the piano. For 7 years, my mom sewed and did all this extra stuff so I could learn to play the piano. There was a missing factor: I didn't have the want at that time.

And so I know with the Cambodian people voting where they were winning these elections and the momentum was with them, to be robbed from that, you know, we have the Cambodian people that are pushing for this. Then you have the Cambodian Government that doesn't want it.

Because what I have seen, you know, countries that are authoritarian, they are afraid of empowering their people. The most valuable resource any country has is their people. It is not their gold, their jade, or any of that other stuff, it is their people. And when you empower their people, they will do well.

Ms. Kem, you brought up that the EU, the United States, Canada, Japan, account for roughly 70—I have got 78 percent of Cambodia's exports. That is a big hand that we can influence better decisions, and that is what our goal is.

And I wish you the best of luck with your father, with the work you guys are doing. I can't tell you how much we appreciate your testimonies. This meeting has gone a little bit long. But everybody has stayed here and this shows you the importance.

Allen, do you have a followup? Any more comments? Dana?

But, again, I can't tell you how much I appreciate it. And it is like I said when I came up to the table. We take the information you give us, we look at different areas where we can give recommendations to the administration, the State Department, or a resolution coming out from the House saying, we stand with these ideals and that we will stand with the support of the Cambodian people.

And then we will also send the information to the Cambodian Government that you either choose to do business with the United States of America following these principles that we have all signed onto, or you do business with somebody else. And I think it is time we start playing that hand, because we see the hand that China is forcing, and it is not in the favor of democracies.

All right. So, with that, this meeting is concluded. I appreciate everybody's participation and have a great day.

[Whereupon, at 3:38 p.m., the subcommittee was adjourned.]

APPENDIX

SUBCOMMITTEE HEARING NOTICE
COMMITTEE ON FOREIGN AFFAIRS
U.S. HOUSE OF REPRESENTATIVES
WASHINGTON, DC 20515-6128

Subcommittee on Asia and the Pacific
Ted Yoho (R-FL), Chairman

December 5, 2017

TO: MEMBERS OF THE COMMITTEE ON FOREIGN AFFAIRS

You are respectfully requested to attend an OPEN hearing of the Committee on Foreign Affairs, to be held by the Subcommittee on Asia and the Pacific in Room 2255 of the Rayburn House Office Building (and available live on the Committee website at http://www.ForeignAffairs.house.gov):

DATE: Tuesday, December 12, 2017

TIME: 2:00 p.m.

SUBJECT: Cambodia's Descent: Policies to Support Democracy and Human Rights

WITNESSES: Ms. Olivia Enos
Policy Analyst
Asian Studies Center
Davis Institute for National Security and Foreign Policy
The Heritage Foundation

Ms. Monovithya Kem
Deputy Director-General of Public Affairs
Cambodia National Rescue Party
(Daughter of Kem Sohka, President, Cambodia National Rescue Party)

Mr. Kenneth Wollack
President
National Democratic Institute

By Direction of the Chairman

The Committee on Foreign Affairs seeks to make its facilities accessible to persons with disabilities. If you are in need of special accommodations, please call 202/225-5021 at least four business days in advance of the event, whenever practicable. Questions with regard to special accommodations in general (including availability of Committee materials in alternative formats and assistive listening devices) may be directed to the Committee.

COMMITTEE ON FOREIGN AFFAIRS

MINUTES OF SUBCOMMITTEE ON ______*Asia and the Pacific*______ HEARING

Day____*Tuesday*____Date__*December 12, 2017*__Room________2255________

Starting Time ____*2:03*____Ending Time ____*3:39*____

Recesses |____| (____to ____) (____to ____) (____to ____) (____to ____) (____to ____) (____to ____)

Presiding Member(s)

Rep. Yoho

Check all of the following that apply:

Open Session [✓]
Executive (closed) Session [ ]
Televised [ ]

Electronically Recorded (taped) [ ]
Stenographic Record [ ]

TITLE OF HEARING:

Cambodia's Descent: Policies to Support Democracy and Human Rights

SUBCOMMITTEE MEMBERS PRESENT:

Rep. Ted Yoho, Rep. Dana Rohrabacher, Rep. Steve Chabot, Rep. Scott Perry, Rep. Mo Brooks Rep. Brad Sherman, Rep. Gerald Connolly

NON-SUBCOMMITTEE MEMBERS PRESENT: *(Mark with an * if they are not members of full committee.)*

Rep. Ed Royce
*Rep. Alan Lowenthal**

HEARING WITNESSES: Same as meeting notice attached? Yes [✓] No [ ]
(If "no", please list below and include title, agency, department, or organization.)

STATEMENTS FOR THE RECORD: *(List any statements submitted for the record.)*

TIME SCHEDULED TO RECONVENE __________
or
TIME ADJOURNED ____*3:39*____

Subcommittee Staff Associate